Food of Culture
"World of Mexico"
Book

#15 of

many more...

A reality series of cookbooks
By Chef Peter Ingrasselino™

I would like to introduce myself my name is Peter Ingrasselino I am a Master Chef. This book is going to bring you on a true reality of what cooking is all about. I am no Author or photographer I am a Chef. I am a realist. This book contains real recipes not mock ups to make you feel like a 5 star chef when you are completed with them but just real down to earth great food from cultures that surround all of us on a daily basis. Have you ever stopped and looked, smelled and wondered what your out of the box food would taste like? Well now is your chance to make it your own and experience what you have been missing out on. The stories are real and they will be told in my words and not corrected, the photos that you will see are actual photos without computerized imaging and clean ups. For me when I see cook books that are so beautiful and artistic and perfect to me that is not the reality, no matter how hard you may try it never comes out like the photo, so my pictures that are in this book are photos from my journey and continuing journey that I am on. I find myself always teaching, showing, having people taste, so I decided to write this book. So enjoy what you read and create, remember it is your creation I am just providing you the tools of creating, the rest is all you.

Mexican Cuisine *Not to be confused with Tex-Mex cuisine, which is often referred to as "Mexican food" in certain regions of the United States* began about 9,000 years ago, when agricultural communities such as the Maya formed, domesticating maize, creating the standard process of maize nixtamalization, and establishing their foodways. Successive waves of other Mesoamerican groups brought with them their own cooking methods. These included the Olmec, Teotihuacanos, Toltec, Huastec, Zapotec, Mixtec, Otomi, Purépecha, Totonac, Mazatec, Mazahua, and Nahua.

The Mexica formation of the Aztec Empire created a multi-ethnic society where many different foodways became infused. The staples are native foods, such as corn (maize), beans, squash, amaranth, chia, avocados, tomatoes, tomatillos, cacao, vanilla, agave, turkey, spirulina, sweet potato, cactus, and chili pepper. After the Spanish conquest of the Aztec Empire in the 16th century and the subsequent conquest of the Maya area, Europeans introduced a number of other foods, the most important of which were meats from domesticated animals (beef, pork, chicken, goat, and sheep), dairy products (especially cheese and milk), and rice. While the Spanish initially tried to impose their own diet on the country, this was not possible.

Asian and African influences were also introduced into the indigenous cuisine during this era as a result of African slavery in New Spain and the Manila-Acapulco Galleons.

Over the centuries, this resulted in regional cuisines based on local conditions, such as those in Oaxaca, Veracruz and the Yucatán Peninsula. Mexican cuisine is an important aspect of the culture, social structure and popular traditions of Mexico. The most important example of this connection is the use of mole for special occasions and holidays, particularly in the South and Central regions of the country.

Mexican cuisine is a complex and ancient cuisine, with techniques and skills developed over thousands of years of history. It is created mostly with ingredients native to Mexico, as well as those brought over by the Spanish conquistadors, with some new influences since then. Mexican cuisine has been influenced by its proximity to the US-Mexican border. For example, burritos were thought to have been invented for easier transportation of beans by wrapping them in tortillas for field labor. Modifications like these brought Mexican cuisine to the United States, where states like Arizona further adapted burritos by deep frying them, creating the modern chimichanga.

In addition to staples, such as corn and chile peppers, native ingredients include tomatoes, squashes, avocados, cocoa and vanilla, as well as ingredients not generally used in other cuisines, such as edible flowers, vegetables like huauzontle and papaloquelite, or small criollo avocados, whose skin is edible. Chocolate originated in Mexico and was prized by the Aztecs. It remains an important ingredient in Mexican cookery.

Vegetables play an important role in Mexican cuisine. Common vegetables include zucchini, cauliflower, corn, potatoes, spinach, Swiss chard, mushrooms, jitomate (red tomato), green tomato, etc. Other traditional vegetable ingredients include Chili pepper, huitlacoche (corn fungus), huauzontle, and nopal (cactus pads) to name a few.

European contributions include pork, chicken, beef, cheese, herbs and spices, as well as some fruits.

Tropical fruits, many of which are indigenous to Mexico and the Americas, such as guava, prickly pear, sapote, mangoes, bananas, pineapple and cherimoya (custard apple) are popular, especially in the center and south of the country.

Edible insects have been enjoyed in Mexico for millennia. Entemophagy or insect-eating is becoming increasingly popular outside of poor and rural areas for its unique flavors, sustainability, and connection to pre-Hispanic heritage. Popular species include chapulines (grasshoppers or crickets), escamoles (ant larvae), cumiles (stink bugs) and ahuatle (water bug eggs).

RECIPES

Ceviche Verde
Homemade Tortilla Chips

Yield: serves 4
Time: 1 hour
For the chips:
6 yellow corn tortillas
4 cups canola oil, for frying
Kosher salt
For the ceviche verde:
7 oz. firm white fish, such as halibut or cod, skin and bones removed
Kosher salt
9 oz. cleaned squid, bodies thinly sliced into rings and tentacles cut into bite-size pieces
4 medium tomatillos (12 oz. total), peeled and rinsed
1 cup cilantro leaves
1 very thinly sliced serrano or jalapeño chile
1 large garlic clove, coarsely chopped
Juice of 6 large limes (about ½ cup)

Instructions

1.   Fry the tortilla chips: Cut each of the tortillas into 4 equal wedges. Line a baking sheet or large platter with a few layers of paper towels.
2.   In a 10-inch stainless-steel skillet, add enough oil to reach about 1 inch up the sides of the pan. Heat until the oil registers 350°F on a deep-fry thermometer. Working in batches of around 6 or 8, add some chips without overcrowding the pan and fry, rotating and turning occasionally with tongs, until deep golden and completely hard and crunchy, do not overcook since this can make the chips too greasy. Transfer to the prepared baking sheet to drain, and immediately sprinkle the chips lightly with salt. Set aside to cool completely while you continue frying the rest.
3.   Make the ceviche: Cut the fish into ½-inch pieces, Set aside.
4.   In a small pot, add enough water to reach three-quarters of the way up the sides of the pot; bring to a boil. Set a medium bowl of ice water next to the stove. Season both waters generously with salt.
5.   Once the water is boiling, add the squid rings and cook until firmed up slightly, 1½ to 2 minutes. Using a slotted spoon, quickly transfer the rings to the ice water to cool. Add the tentacles to the boiling water and repeat; remove to the ice water. Remove all of the squid from the water when completely chilled, pat dry, and refrigerate.
6.   In a blender, add the tomatillos, cilantro, chile, garlic, and a generous pinch of salt; pulse until runny but still slightly chunky.
7.   In a fine-mesh strainer set over a medium bowl, strain the tomatillo mixture, reserving the liquid and the solids.
8.   When ready to serve, in a shallow, medium serving bowl, add the fish, squid, and lime juice; stir well. Stir in the solids from the tomatillo mixture plus 2–3 tablespoons of the reserved liquid. Let stand, stirring occasionally, for 5 minutes. Taste and adjust the seasoning or consistency with more salt, lime juice, or tomatillo liquid as needed. Serve immediately with the chips.

Mexican Street Corn Soup

Yield: serves 6
Time: 1 hour, 30 minutes
Ingredients
8 medium ears corn (3 lb. 12 oz.), shucked
4 Tbsp. (2 oz.) unsalted butter
1 medium yellow onion, finely chopped (1½ cups)
1 rib celery, finely chopped (½ cup)
1 medium poblano pepper, seeded, stemmed, and finely chopped
(½ cup)
4 cloves garlic, finely chopped (1 Tbsp. plus 1 tsp.)
1 tsp. dried Mexican oregano
1 fresh bay leaf
3½ cups whole milk
3 medium yellow potatoes (about 1½ lb.), peeled and cut into ½-
inch pieces
1 cup heavy cream
Kosher salt
1 Tbsp. ancho chile powder, plus more for topping
¼ cups thinly sliced cilantro
½ cups Mexican crema or sour cream
½ cups crumbled cotija cheese
Lime wedges, for serving

Instructions

1.   On a medium-hot grill or hot grill pan, char the corn all over, 15–20 minutes. Transfer to a platter and set aside until cool enough to handle.

2.   Working over a large bowl, slice the corn kernels off each cob, scraping the cob with the knife to extract the flavorful juices. Halve 5 of the bare corn cobs crosswise, discarding the rest. Set the kernels and cobs aside.

3.   In a medium pot over medium heat, melt the butter. When the foam begins to subside, add the onion, celery, poblano, garlic, oregano, and bay leaf. Cover and cook, stirring occasionally, until the onion softens, 7–8 minutes. Add the reserved corn kernels and cobs, milk, potatoes, and cream. Bring to a boil, cover, and lower the heat to maintain a simmer. Cook, stirring occasionally, until the potatoes are tender, about 25 minutes. Remove and discard the cobs and bay leaf. Transfer 1½ cups of the soup to a blender and purée until smooth. Stir the puréed soup back into the pot of remaining soup to thicken. Season with salt and the ancho chile powder, then ladle into wide soup bowls and garnish with the cilantro, crema, cotija, and additional ancho chile powder. Serve with lime wedges.

Fried Shredded Beef Empanadas

Yield: makes 8
Time: 2 hours, 45 minutes
For the filling
1 lb. trimmed beef shoulder
Salt
3 cloves garlic
1 bay leaf
1 large white onion, half coarsely chopped
1/4 cup canola or rice bran oil
1/4 cup dried árbol chiles, stemmed and seeded
4 large dried guajillo chiles, stemmed and seeded
2 medium tomatillos, husked and rinsed
For the empanadas
2 cups Homemade Masa, or masa prepared from store-bought
masa harina
2 tbsp. lard
1/2 tsp. baking powder
Canola oil or rice bran oil, for frying Your choice of garnishes such
as sliced green cabbage, cilantro, hot sauce, crumbled queso
fresco, and sour cream

Instructions

1. Make the filling: Place the beef in a medium pot and season all over with salt. Add 2 garlic cloves, the bay leaf, the unchopped half of the onion, and enough water just to cover the meat. Bring to a boil, then reduce to a simmer and let cook until tender, 1 1/2-2 hours. Let cool slightly. Finely shred the meat and season generously with salt (discard the broth).

2. Meanwhile, in a large skillet heat the oil over medium-high heat until hot. Add all of the chiles and cook, turning frequently with tongs, until bright red and lightly toasted in places, 15-20 seconds (do not overcook or chiles will be bitter); remove and transfer to a heatproof bowl. Cover with boiling water and let sit until softened, 20 minutes.

3. Transfer the chiles to a blender, adding only a little of the soaking water as needed to help blend. Add the remaining garlic clove, the tomatillos, the chopped onion, and a generous pinch of salt and purée until smooth. Combine the salsa with the shredded beef, starting with just enough to moisten the meat and adding more to taste; do not overmoisten. (Meat and salsa can be prepared up to 2 days ahead.)

4. Make the empanadas: In the bowl of a stand mixer fitted with the paddle attachment, mix the masa with the lard and baking powder until well combined. (Alternatively, you can stir the ingredients by hand in a large bowl, but the mixer will produce lighter, airier empanada shells.)

5.   To form the empanadas, line a tortilla press with two small rounds of parchment paper or plastic cut from a plastic bag to fit. Scoop out 1/4 cup of masa dough and form it tightly into a ball, then flatten the ball slightly into a tight disk. Place the disk in the center of the tortilla press, sandwiched between the two rounds of plastic. Close the press to form a large round slightly thicker than a tortilla (about 1/8 inch thick when raw; the dough will expand in the fryer). Carefully peel away the top liner. Holding the pressed masa round in one hand atop the plastic round, place some of the beef filling (a scant 1/4 cup) at its center, leaving a generous border. Using the remaining piece of plastic to support the delicate masa, carefully fold the empanada shell in half to cover the filling and form a half-moon shape. Press the joined edges of the pastry together to seal tightly. Transfer to a parchment paper-lined baking sheet or platter and repeat with the remaining masa and filling.

6.   Set a plate lined with paper towels next to the stove. In a 12-inch skillet, add enough oil to come 1 inch up the sides of the pan. Heat the oil until a deep-fry thermometer reads 350° or a small piece of masa dropped into the center bubbles vigorously. Working in batches of 2-3 as needed, carefully place the empanadas in the pan; cook until lightly browned, about 4 minutes, then turn and repeat. Transfer to the prepared plate and season with salt. Serve garnished with your choice of cabbage, cilantro, hot sauce, queso fresco, and sour cream.

Some Random Pics...

Corn Tamales with Tomatillo Salsa

Yield: makes 1 cup
Time: 5 minutes

Ingredients

8 large tomatillos, husked and rinsed
2 tbsp. freshly squeezed lime juice
1/4 tsp. kosher salt
1 jalapeño, coarsely chopped (optional)in a blender, combine the tomatillos, lime juice, salt, and jalapeño (if using); blend until slightly chunky and you can still see the seeds.

Instructions

1.   In a blender, combine the tomatillos, lime juice, salt, and jalapeño (if using); blend until slightly chunky and you can still see the seeds. Spoon over corn tamales.

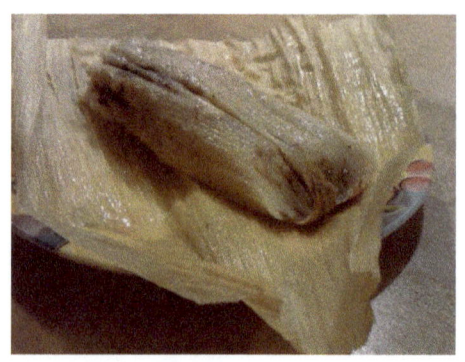

Some Random Pics...

www.drehmomente.com.de

19

Homemade Masa

Yield: makes 5 cups
Time: 8 hours, 45 minutes
Ingredients
4 cups dried corn (about 1 1/2 lb.)
3 tbsp. calcium hydroxide (also called "cal" or pickling lime)
Salt

NOTES

Instructions

1. In a large pot, add the corn and enough water to cover it by double (8-10 cups). Stir in the cal and bring the water to a low boil. Let cook, stirring every 5 minutes to check the water content, until the corn is al dente (when broken or bitten, the center of the kernel will still be slightly white) and the silky skins slip off easily when rubbed between fingers, 5-20 minutes. Turn off the heat and add water as needed to cover the corn by 2 inches. Cover and let rest at least 8 hours and up to 16 hours (corn will have swelled in size and may have changed color).

2. Transfer to a strainer and wash the corn under cold running water, rubbing it vigorously between your hands, until most of the skins have come off and the kernels look shiny (don't use a fine-mesh strainer, as you want the skins to fall to the bottom of the strainer or slip away through the holes). Use the corn immediately or store fully covered in fresh, cool water for up to 1 day in the refrigerator.

3. Grind the corn on nearly the tightest setting in a *molino de mano* (hand-operated corn grinder), pouring 1-2 teaspoons water over corn as needed to help it slide through the grinder. Tighten the setting all the way and repeat the grinding. If making tortillas, grind the masa once more in a stone grinder (*metate*) to get a fine, smooth consistency. Season with salt and add small amounts of water only as needed to reach a moist but not sticky consistency. Chill in a roomy container and use within 2 days. Bring to room temperature before using.

Enchiladas

Yield: makes 12
Ingredients
8 dried New Mexico chiles, stemmed and seeded
1 oz. Mexican chocolate, such as Ibarra, roughly chopped
1/2 tsp. dried oregano
1/4 tsp. ground cinnamon
4 saltine crackers or 2 1/2 tbsp. bread crumbs
1 clove garlic
1 whole clove
1/2 cup plus 1 tbsp. canola oil
Kosher salt, to taste
2 cups queso añejo, grated, plus more to garnish 1/2 small yellow
onion, minced
12 corn tortillas

NOTES

Instructions

1.   Make the red chile sauce: Heat chiles in a 12″ skillet over high heat, and cook, turning as needed, until toasted, about 5 minutes; transfer chiles to a blender with chocolate, oregano, cinnamon, crackers, garlic, clove, and 1 1/2 cups boiling water, and let sit for 5 minutes. Puree until smooth, and then pour sauce through a fine strainer into a bowl.

2.   Heat 1 tbsp. oil in a 2-qt. saucepan over medium-high heat, and add chile sauce; cook, stirring often, until reduced and thickened, about 6 minutes. Season with salt and set aside.

3.   To assemble the enchiladas, combine the queso añejo and onion in a small bowl and set aside. Pour oil to a depth of 2″ in a 6-qt. Dutch oven and heat over medium-high heat until a deep-fry thermometer reads 350°.

4.   Using tongs, grasp all the tortillas in a stack and submerge in oil, swirling in oil until slightly fried and pliable, about 15 seconds. (The surface of the tortillas should puff up in tiny pockets in several places.) Remove from oil and set aside on a plate to cool. (Alternatively, you may wrap the tortillas in a damp towel towel and briefly microwave to steam.)

5.   Dip each tortilla in chile sauce until completely coated. Transfer to a plate and top with 3 tbsp. cheese filling; roll up like a cigar and sprinkle with more cheese. Serve immediately with rice and beans.

Hatch Green Chile Enchiladas

Yield: serves 6

For the Chicken and Sauce

1 (3 1/2 lb.) chicken, with the neck, but giblets removed

1 small carrot (3 oz.)

1 large white onion (10 oz.)

3 unpeeled garlic cloves

1/2 tsp. cumin seed

2 tbsp. unsalted butter

2 cups diced white onion

4 garlic cloves, minced

2 tbsp. all-purpose flour

3 cups roasted, peeled and chopped Hatch green chiles (from about 30 if using fresh chiles)

6 cups hot chicken broth (see below)

Salt and pepper

1/4 tsp. dried oregano

For the Enchiladas and Garnish

12 soft corn tortillas

2 1/2 cups (7 oz.) grated Oaxacan or Monterey Jack cheese, or a mix

2 cups (10 oz.) crumbled queso fresco

4 scallions, thinly sliced (3/4 cup)

1 cup coarsely chopped cilantro leaves and tender stems (from about 1 bunch)

Crema, crème fraîche, or sour cream

Thinly slivered crisp lettuce, tomato slices and radishes (optional)

Instructions

1.   Make the chicken: In a large pot or Dutch oven, add the chicken, chicken neck and enough water just to cover. Add the carrot, onion, and garlic cloves and bring to a simmer. Let simmer until the meat is cooked through and the broth is flavorful, about 40 minutes.

2.   Strain, reserving both the broth and the chicken. (If desired, you can continue to simmer the chicken neck and vegetables in the stock to further concentrate the flavor while the chicken cools, another 30 minutes.) Let the chicken rest until cool enough to handle. Shred the meat and discard the bones and skin. You should have 4 cups meat. Set aside. Reserve 6 cups of broth for the sauce, plus 2 cups more for softening tortillas.

3.   Make the sauce: In a small, dry skillet over medium-high heat, add the cumin. Cook, stirring or shaking the pan occasionally, until fragrant, about 3 minutes. Remove, then finely grind.

4.   In a large saucepan over medium-high heat, melt the butter. Once hot, add the onions and cook, stirring occasionally, until softened and barely colored, about 8 minutes. Stir in the minced garlic and let cook 1 minute, then sprinkle the flour into the pan and stir to incorporate. Add the chiles. Season generously with salt and lightly with black pepper, then add the cumin and oregano; stir well. Gradually whisk in the chicken broth and bring to a simmer. Simmer for 10 minutes (sauce should thicken slightly). Taste and adjust the seasoning as needed, then set aside. (Sauce and chicken can be prepared up to 1 day ahead. Cover and refrigerate.)

5.   Make the enchiladas: Preheat the oven to 400°. Ladle 1 1/2 cups of the sauce into a 9-by-13-inch glass baking dish. Heat the remaining chicken broth (alternatively, prepare a steamer). To soften the tortillas so they can be rolled without breaking, dip them very briefly in the hot broth, or steam them, until softened slightly. (Traditionally, tortillas are lightly fried to soften.)

6.   Working one at a time, distribute about 3 tablespoons of the shredded chicken down the center of each tortilla. Roll the tortilla loosely into a cigar shape to cover the filling, then transfer seam side down to the prepared baking dish. Repeat with the remaining tortillas and chicken, placing the enchiladas snugly side by side. Ladle the remaining sauce over the top to coat generously. Sprinkle the cheese atop the sauce, cover with foil and bake until the enchiladas are heated through and the sauce is beginning to bubble, about 20 minutes. Remove the foil and bake until the top is browned and bubbling, 15-20 minutes more.

7.   Remove the enchiladas and sprinkle with the queso fresco, scallions, and cilantro, Divide among 6 individual plates and drizzle or dollop each portion generously with crema or sour cream. Garnish each with the lettuce, tomato and radish, if using. Serve immediately.

NOTES

Some Random Pics...

Coconut Horchata

Yield: serves 4
Time: 5 minutes
Ingredients
2 cups boiling water
2 cups long-grain white rice
1 stick cinnamon, crushed, plus sticks for garnish
2 cups unsweetened coconut water
Cheesecloth, for straining
1 cup unsweetened coconut milk
2/3 cup sugar
1 pinch kosher salt
Instructions

1.   Stir water, rice, and cinnamon in a bowl; cover and let sit at room temperature overnight.
2.   The next day, transfer rice mixture to a blender. Add coconut water; purée until smooth, 3–4 minutes. Strain through a cheesecloth-lined sieve into a pitcher; cover and chill until ready to serve.
3.   Heat coconut milk, sugar, and salt in a 2-qt. saucepan over low; cook until sugar dissolves, about 3 minutes. Let milk cool; stir into rice mixture. Serve in ice-filled glasses; grate fresh cinnamon over top and drop sticks into glasses.

Some Random Pics...

Shrimp Tacos

Yield: serves 6
Time: 1 hour, 30 minutes
For the Rice
1 1/2 cups chicken stock
2 plum tomatoes, cored and roughly chopped
2 tbsp. canola oil
2 cloves garlic, minced
1 small white onion, minced
1 cup long-grain white rice
Kosher salt and freshly ground black pepper, to taste
For the Shrimp and Serving
1 1/2 lb. medium shrimp, peeled and deveined, tails removed
1 tsp. Worcestershire sauce
2 cloves garlic, minced
1 lime, juiced
Kosher salt and freshly ground black pepper, to taste
2 tbsp. canola oil
Flour tortillas, warmed, for serving
<u>Chiles de Árbol Salsa and Guacamole</u>, for serving
Shredded jack cheese, for serving
Roughly chopped cilantro and white onion, for garnish
Lime wedges, for serving

Instructions

1. Make the rice: Purée stock and tomatoes in a blender until smooth; set aside. Heat oil in a 4-qt. saucepan over medium-high. Cook garlic and onion until soft, about 5 minutes. Add rice; cook until golden, about 6 minutes. Stir in reserved tomato mixture, salt, and pepper; boil. Reduce heat to low; cook, covered, until rice is tender, 25–30 minutes. Remove from heat and let sit, covered, for 10 minutes.

2. Make the shrimp: Stir shrimp, Worcestershire, garlic, lime juice, salt, and pepper in a bowl; let sit 10 minutes. Wipe skillet clean; heat oil over medium-high. Working in batches, cook shrimp until pink and cooked through, 2–3 minutes. To serve, divide rice and shrimp between tortillas; top with reserved salsa and guacamole, the cheese, cilantro, and onion. Serve with lime wedges.

Chicken Quesadillas

Yield: serves 4-6
Time: 30 minutes
Ingredients
1 tsp. ground cumin
1 tsp. chili powder
1 tsp. garlic powder
1 tsp. ground coriander
1 tsp. kosher salt, plus more to taste
1 tsp. onion powder
1 tsp. smoked paprika
1/2 tsp. dried oregano
1 1/4 lb. boneless skinless chicken breasts (about 2)
1/2 cup olive oil
1 orange bell pepper, seeded and thinly sliced
1 red bell pepper, seeded and thinly sliced
1 yellow bell pepper, seeded and thinly sliced
1 medium red onion, 1/4 minced, the rest thinly sliced
1 avocado
2 tbsp. fresh lime juice
1 tbsp. minced cilantro
1 tomato, cored, seeded, and minced
Freshly ground black pepper, to taste
10 flour tortillas
8 oz. shredded cheddar cheese
8 oz. shredded Monterey Jack cheese
4 oz. queso fresco
Sour cream, to serve

Instructions

1. Combine cumin, chili powder, garlic powder, coriander, salt, onion powder, paprika, and oregano in a bowl; mix half with the chicken. Heat 3 tbsp. oil in a 12-inch skillet over medium-high; cook chicken, flipping once, until half way cooked, about 8 minutes. Add remaining seasoning, peppers, sliced onion, and salt and cook until peppers are soft and chicken is cooked through, about 8 minutes more. Transfer chicken to a cutting board and rest 10 minutes before thinly slicing.

2. Cut avocado in half lengthwise, then remove and discard pit. Make crosshatch incisions in avocado pulp with a paring knife. Scoop pulp out with a spoon, then transfer to a bowl with minced onion, lime juice, cilantro, tomato, salt, and pepper; mix. Chill guacamole until ready to use.

3. Working in batches, heat 1 tablespoon oil in a 12-inch nonstick skillet; place one tortilla in the skillet. Top with 3 tablespoons of both cheddar and Monterey Jack; place 1/5 of onion and pepper mixture and some slices of chicken on top. Finish with 1-2 tablespoons more of each cheese and some queso fresco, as well as another tortilla. Cook for 2 minutes, until golden, then flip over and cook a further 1-2 minutes until the other side is golden and the cheese has melted. Transfer to a cutting board and slice into 6 pieces. Serve with guacamole and sour cream.

Sopa Azteca
Mexican Chicken Tortilla Soup

Yield: serves 4-6
Time: 45 minutes
Ingredients
1 large pasilla chile
1 (15-oz.) can diced tomatoes
2 tbsp. canola oil
3 cloves garlic, peeled
1 medium white onion, roughly chopped
8 cups chicken stock
1 epazote or cilantro sprig (optional)
1 1/2 lb. boneless, skinless chicken breast, cut into 1/2-inch pieces
Kosher salt and freshly ground black pepper
6 oz. shredded Monterey Jack cheese
1-2 avocados, diced
Crema or sour cream, for serving
Lime wedges, for serving
Tortilla chips (about 4 cups), crushed, for serving

Instructions

1.   Toast the chile in a 6-quart saucepan over high heat, turning, until fragrant (alternatively, toast it over an open flame for a few seconds). Remove the stem and seeds and break the chile into pieces; transfer to a blender along with the tomatoes.

2.   Heat oil in saucepan and cook garlic and onion until golden, 8-10 minutes. Using a slotted spoon, transfer garlic and onion to blender with the tomatoes and chile and purée until smooth.

3.   Pour tomato mixture into saucepan and cook over medium-high until thick, 8-10 minutes. Add the stock and epazote, if using, and boil. Reduce the heat to medium-low and simmer for 15 minutes. Add the chicken, salt, and pepper and cook until chicken is cooked through, about 8 minutes more. Divide tortilla chips between bowls and ladle soup over; top with cheese, avocado, more tortilla chips, and crema. Serve with lime wedges on the side.

Guacamole

Ingredients
1/4 cup chopped cilantro, divided
2 tbsp. finely chopped white onion
1/2 tsp. kosher salt
1/2 fresh serrano chile, stemmed and finely chopped
1 lb. avocados (about 2 small), halved and pitted
2 tbsp. fresh lime juice
Tortilla chips, for serving

Instructions
1. Mash half the cilantro, the onion, salt, and serrano into a paste in a mortar and pestle. Scoop out the flesh of the avocado and roughly chop; add to mortar along with remaining cilantro and lime juice and lightly mash. Serve with tortilla chips.

Some Random Pics...

Shrimp and Chorizo Sausage

Yield: makes about 2 pounds
Time: 1 hour, 30 minutes
Ingredients
2 tbsp. dried Mexican oregano
2 tsp. coriander seeds
2 tsp. whole black peppercorns
2 bay leaves
2 whole cloves
1 cinnamon stick
10 cloves garlic
10 guajillo chiles, stemmed and seeded
1 1/2 cups heavy cream
2 tbsp. granulated sugar
1 tbsp. kosher salt
1 egg white
20 oz. peeled and deveined shrimp (about 40), minced

NOTES

Instructions

1.   Heat a medium skillet over medium-high; toast oregano, coriander, peppercorns, bay leaves, cloves, and cinnamon until fragrant, about 30 seconds. Transfer to a spice grinder and pulse into a fine powder.

2.   Heat skillet over medium and cook garlic and chiles, turning as needed, until blackened in spots, about 5 minutes. Remove from heat and transfer chiles to a bowl; cover with boiling water and soak for 30 minutes. Peel garlic and transfer cloves to a food processor along with spice powder, cream, sugar, salt, and egg white. Drain chiles, discarding liquid, and add to food processor; purée until smooth. Transfer mixture to a bowl with shrimp and mix until combined.

Mexican Ricotta Croquettes

Yield: makes 12
Time: 1 hour, 15 minutes
For the Chipotle-Honey Salsa:
4 plum tomatoes, cored
1 garlic clove, peeled
1/2 large yellow onion, roughly chopped
1 tbsp. vegetable oil
kosher salt
3 tbsp. honey
1 tsp. rice vinegar
2 cilantro sprigs
1 (7-ounce) can chipotle chiles in adobo sauce
For the Ricotta Latkes:
1 cup requeson (Mexican ricotta) or ricotta cheese
1 cup queso cremita, such as Tropical brand
1 cup finely crumbled cotija cheese
1 cup Chihuahua or mozzarella cheese
1/2 cup softened cream cheese
1/2 cup matzo meal
2 sticks unsalted butter, melted
2 large eggs
1 cup plain bread crumbs
vegetable oil, for frying

Instructions

1. Make the chipotle-honey salsa: Heat the broiler. In a roasting pan, combine the tomatoes with the garlic and onion, then toss with the oil and season with salt. Broil, turning the vegetables as needed, until lightly blackened all over, about 6 minutes. Remove from oven and let cool. Transfer the vegetables to a food processor along with the honey, vinegar, cilantro, and chiles and adobo sauce and pulse until smooth.

2. Make the latkes: In a large bowl, combine the all 5 cheese with the matzo meal, butter and eggs and then refrigerate for 30 minutes. Using a 1-inch ice cream scoop, portion out balls of cheese, roll them in your hands to smooth, then coat them in the bread crumbs.

3. Pour enough oil into a 6-qt. Dutch oven to come 2 inches up the side and heat to 350° on a deep-fry thermometer. Working with 6 balls at a time, add the latkes to the oil and cook until golden brown, 1 to 2 minutes. Drain the latkes on paper towels and serve immediately with the chipotle-honey salsa.

Whitefish Guacamole

Yield: serves 4
Time: 15 minutes
Ingredients
5 tbsp. minced red onion
2 tbsp. plus 1 tsp. finely chopped cilantro
1 jalapeño, stemmed, seeded, and finely chopped
juice of 1 lime
1 cup smoked whitefish
1 tbsp. mayonnaise
1 1/2 tsp. adobo sauce from a can of chipotles in adobo sauce
1 tsp. minced chives
2 avocados, halved, pitted, peeled and roughly chopped
kosher salt
Instructions
1.   In a large bowl, stir the onion, cilantro, jalapeno, and lime juice together and let stand for 5 minutes. Add the whitefish, mayonnaise, adobo sauce, chives, and avocados and stir until evenly combined. Serve the guacamole with tortilla chips.

Some Random Pics...

Brisket Tacos

Yield: serves 8
Time: 4 hours
For the Brisket:
1/4 cup vegetable oil
2 lb. lean beef brisket
kosher salt and freshly ground black pepper
1 cup finely chopped carrot
1 cup finely chopped celery
1 cup finely chopped yellow onion
5 garlic cloves, peeled
2 cups canned tomato puree
2 tbsp. adobo sauce from a can of chipotles in adobo
1/4 tsp. ground cumin
1/4 tsp. dried Mexican oregano
5 thyme sprigs
1 bay leaf
1 (12-ounce) bottle Mexican beer
For the Tomatillo Salsa:
1/2 cup cilantro leaves, plus more, finely chopped, for serving
5 medium-to-large tomatillos, husks removed then quartered
2 garlic cloves, peeled
2 jalapeños, stemmed, seeded, and cut lengthwise into 8 strips
each
1 small yellow onion, peeled and quartered
1 avocado, halved, pitted, peeled, and cut lengthwise into 12
wedges
8 (5") corn tortillas, warmed
lime wedge and finely chopped red onion, for serving

Instructions

1.   Make the brisket: Heat the oven to 325°. In a large saucepan, heat the oil over medium-high. Season the brisket with salt and pepper, then add to the pan, and cook, turning as needed, until browned all over, about 12 minutes. Transfer the brisket to a plate and return the pan to medium heat.

2.   Add the carrot, celery, onion, and garlic, and cook, stirring, for 5 minutes. Add the tomato puree, adobo sauce, cumin, oregano, and bay leaf and cook, stirring, for 2 minutes. Stir in the beer, then return the brisket to the pot and pour enough water into the pot to cover the meat and bring it to a boil. Cover with the lid and bake until the brisket is very tender, about 2 1/2 hours. Transfer the pan to a rack and let the brisket cool in the cooking liquid.

3.   Once cooled, remove the brisket from liquid and shred with two forks. Pour the braising liquid into a blender and puree until smooth. Return the liquid to the pot over medium heat, stir in the shredded brisket, and reheat until warmed through.

4.   Meanwhile, make the tomatillo salsa: In a blender, puree the cilantro with the tomatillos, garlic, jalapenos, yellow onion, and avocado, and season with salt.

5.   Serve the brisket in the tortillas and top with a drizzle of the tomatillo salsa and the red onions, chopped cilantro, and lime wedges.

Mexican Braised Spare Ribs Squash and Corn

Yield: serves 4 to 6 people
Time: 2 hours, 30 minutes
Ingredients
5 poblano chiles
1/2 lb. tomatoes
2 garlic cloves
1 yellow onion
1 1/2 lb. pork spare-ribs
Kosher salt and freshly ground black pepper
2 tbsp. lard
1 1/2 lb. zucchini, trimmed, halved lengthwise and sliced on the bias
3 ears of corn, kernels removed and saved, cob thrown away
4 cups beef stock
1/2 lb. firm Mexican cheese, for serving

Instructions

1. Heat the oven to broil. Place poblanos on a baking sheet and cook, turning as needed, until charred, about 15 minutes. Set aside to cool slightly, then trim, remove the seeds, and thinly slice.

2. Meanwhile, cover tomatoes, garlic, and onion with water and bring to a boil. Reduce heat to a simmer and cook until the tomatoes are soft, 5 minutes. Drain, discarding liquid, place tomatoes, garlic, and onion in a blender, and purée until smooth.

3. Heat the lard in a large saucepan over medium-high. Season ribs with salt and pepper and, working in batches, cook, turning as needed, until browned, about 6 minutes, and transfer the ribs to a plate. Add the reserved tomato purée, the zucchini, and the corn to the pan and cook, stirring, until most of the liquid has evaporated, about 5 minutes. Add the stock and the ribs and cook, uncovered, until thick and the ribs are tender, about 1 1/2 hours. Serve on a platter.

Masa Ball and Tomato Soup

Ingredients
1 lb. stale tortillas, torn
1 cup milk
2 oz. grated cotija cheese
6 epazote leaves, roughly chopped
1 garlic clove
1 small white onion, roughly chopped
1 large egg plus 1 yolk
3 oz. lard
1/2 cup heavy cream
8 cups beef stock
6 tbsp. tomato purée
Kosher salt and freshly ground black pepper

Instructions
1. In a large bowl, soak the tortillas in the milk until soft, about 30 minutes. Transfer to a food processor along with the cheese, epazote, garlic, onion, egg and yolk, salt, and pepper and purée until smooth. Roll the mixture into 2-inch balls.
2. Heat lard in a large saucepan over medium-high. Cook the tortilla balls, turning as needed, until golden, 5 minutes. Transfer balls to a plate and set aside.
3. Add the tomato purée and cook 2 to 3 minutes. Add the beef stock, salt, and pepper and boil simmer for 10 minutes. Add the tortillas balls and cream and cook 5 minutes more.

Some Random Pics...

Cochinita Pibil Tacos Yacatan-Style Shredded pork Tacos with Achiote

Yield: serves 8-10
Time: 4 hours
Ingredients

4 oz. achiote paste, such as El Yucateco (mexgrocer.com)

1 cup fresh lime juice

1 cup fresh orange juice

1 1/3 cups white vinegar

3 tbsp. dried oregano, preferably Mexican (mexgrocer.com)

2 tsp. Kosher salt, plus more, to taste

4 lb. boneless pork shoulder, cut into 2" pieces

2 (28"-long) banana leaves

2 cups boiling water

1 medium red onion, thinly sliced

4 cloves garlic, thinly sliced

2 habanero peppers, thinly sliced

1 bay leaf

Corn tortillas, warmed, for serving

Roughly chopped cilantro, sliced radishes, and lime wedges, for serving

Instructions

1.   Make the pork: Combine achiote paste, lime and orange juices, 1/3 cup vinegar, and the oregano in a blender; season with salt and purée until smooth. Strain marinade through a fine-mesh sieve into a bowl; add pork and toss to combine. Line the bottom of a 6-qt. Dutch oven with banana leaves, letting the excess hang over the side of the pot. Add pork and its marinade; fold leaves over pork and place lid on pot; bring to a boil. Reduce heat to medium-low; cook until pork is tender, about 2 1/2 hours.

2.   Meanwhile, stir water and onion in a bowl; let sit 3 minutes and drain. Stir in remaining vinegar, 2 tsp. salt, the garlic, habaneros, and bay leaf; cover and let sit at room temperature for at least 1 hour before serving.

3.   Unwrap and transfer pork to a cutting board; shred into bite-size pieces and transfer to a bowl. Stir in 1 cup cooking liquid from the pot. To serve, divide pork between tortillas; top with pickled onion mixture, the cilantro, and radishes. Serve with lime wedges.

Carne Adobada
Red Chile and Pork Stew

Yield: serves 8-10

Ingredients

5 oz. dried New Mexico chiles, stemmed
2 tbsp. New Mexico chile powder
2 tbsp. honey
1 tbsp. white wine vinegar
2 tsp. ground cumin
1 1/2 tsp. ground cloves
1/8 tsp. cayenne pepper
Juice of 1/2 lime
5 tbsp. olive oil
3 lb. boneless pork shoulder, cut into 1 1/2″ chunks
Kosher salt and freshly ground blackpepper, to taste
Warm corn tortillas, for serving

Instructions

1.   Heat chiles in a 6-qt. Dutch oven over medium-high heat, and cook, turning once, until toasted, about 5 minutes; transfer to a large bowl, cover with 8 cups boiling water, and let sit for 20 minutes. Drain chiles, reserving 1 1/2 cups soaking liquid, and transfer chiles to a blender along with reserved soaking liquid, chile powder, honey, vinegar, cumin, cloves, cayenne, and lime juice. Puree until smooth and set sauce aside.

2.   Return pot to medium-high heat and add oil; season pork with salt and pepper, and working in batches, add pork to pot and cook until browned on all sides, about 12 minutes. Add sauce and bring to a boil; reduce heat to medium-low and cook, stirring occasionally, until liquid is thickened and pork is tender, about 1 1/2 hours. Serve with warm corn tortillas.

Some Random Pics...

Goat Birria
Jalisco-Style Goat Stew

Yield: serves 6-8
Time: 3 hours, 30 minutes
Ingredients
1 dried guajillo chile, stemmed
1 cup boiling water
8 tomatillos, husked and cored
5 cloves garlic, unpeeled
1 medium white onion, havled (one half minced)
1 serrano chile, stemmed
1/4 cup cider vinegar
2 tsp. dried oregano, preferably Mexican
1/2 tsp. ground cinnamon
1/2 tsp. ground cumin
1/4 tsp. freshly ground black pepper
1 (2") piece ginger, peeled and thinly sliced
2 tbsp. canola oil
3 lb. bone-in goat shoulder, cut into 3" pieces (ask your
butcher to do this)
Kosher salt, to taste
1 1/2 cups chicken stock
1/2 cup roughly chopped cilantro
Corn tortillas, warmed, for serving
Lime wedges, for serving

Instructions

1.   Heat a 6-qt. Dutch oven over medium-high. Add guajillo chile; cook, flipping once, until lightly toasted, 3–4 minutes. Transfer to a blender, add water, and let sit until soft, about 30 minutes. Remove chile, discard stem and seeds, and return to blender; set aside.

2.   Return pot to medium-high; cook tomatillos, garlic, whole onion half, and serrano, turning as needed, until blackened all over, 12–15 minutes. Peel garlic and transfer to blender with remaining charred vegetables. Add vinegar, oregano, cinnamon, cumin, pepper, and ginger; purée until smooth.

3.   Add oil to pan; heat over medium-high. Season goat with salt and, working in batches, cook, turning as needed, until browned, 18–20 minutes. Transfer goat to a bowl; set aside. Add minced onion; cook until soft, 2–3 minutes. Add reserved chile sauce; simmer until thickened, 4–6 minutes. Return goat to pan and add stock; boil. Reduce heat to medium; simmer, covered and stirring occasionally, until goat is tender, about 2 hours. Using a slotted spoon, transfer goat to a cutting board. Let cool slightly; shred meat, discarding bones, and return to pan. Stir in cilantro; serve with tortillas and lime wedges.

Chile de Arbol Salsa

Yield: makes About 1 Cup
Ingredients
2 tbsp. canola oil
4 cloves garlic
1/4 white onion, chopped
55 dried chile de arbol, stems removed
1 tomato, roughly chopped
Kosher salt, to taste
Instructions
1.   Heat oil in a 12" skillet over medium-high; cook garlic until brown, 3 minutes. Add onion and cook 3 minutes more. Add chiles and cook 1-2 minutes. Add tomatoes and 1/4 cup water; cook until tomatoes begin to break down, 8-10 minutes. Place in a blender with salt and 10 tbsp. water; purée until smooth.

Some Random Pics...

Sopa de Chile Ancho
Ancho Chile Soup with Avocado, Crema, and Chile Pasilla

Yield: serves 6-8
Ingredients
3 dried ancho chiles
4 medium plum tomatoes
2 cloves garlic
1 small white onion
1/2 cup canola oil
8 small dried pasilla chiles
8 cups chicken stock
Kosher salt and freshly ground black pepper, to taste
1 cup queso fresco, crumbled
8 sprigs cilantro, finely chopped
1/2 cup crema or sour cream
1 avocado, very thinly sliced
Fried tortilla strips, for garnish

Instructions

1.   Heat a 6-qt. Dutch oven over medium-high heat. Add ancho chiles, and cook, turning once, until lightly toasted, about 5 minutes. Transfer to a bowl, pour over 1 cup boiling water, and let sit until soft, about 30 minutes; drain chiles, reserving soaking liquid, and remove and discard stems and seeds. Transfer chiles to a blender and set aside. Return pot to heat, and add tomatoes, garlic, and onion; cook, turning as needed, until blackened all over, about 10 minutes. Transfer to blender, and puree until smooth, at least 4 minutes. Pour through a fine strainer into a bowl, and set chile puree aside.

2.   Return saucepan to heat and add 1/4 cup oil; add pasilla chiles, if using, and fry, turning once, until crisp, about 5 minutes. Transfer to paper towels and let cool. Discard oil and wipe pan clean.

3.   Return pan to medium-high heat, and add remaining oil. When hot, add chile puree, and fry, stirring constantly, until slightly reduced, about 6 minutes. Add stock, and bring to a boil; remove from heat, season with salt and pepper, and keep warm.

4.   Divide cheese and cilantro among serving bowls, and then ladle soup over each. Top each with a dollop of crema, a few slices of avocado, and some tortilla strips; garnish with a fried pasilla chile, if you like.

Mango with Cilantro, Coconut, and Chile Powder

Yield: serves 6-8
Time: 10 minutes
Ingredients
3 ripe mangos, peeled, pitted, and sliced into cubes
3 tbsp. fresh lime juice
1 tsp. New Mexican chile powder
1/4 tsp. kosher salt
1/3 cup packed cilantro leaves
1/3 cup shaved unsweetened coconut
Instructions
1.   Arrange mango in an even layer on a serving platter. Sprinkle with lime juice, chile powder, and salt. Garnish with cilantro and coconut.

Some Random Pics...

Chilaquiles

Yield: serves 6
Ingredients
6 plum tomatoes, cored
2 cloves garlic, unpeeled
1 jalapeño, stemmed, halved lengthwise, and seeded
1 small white onion, quartered
2 tbsp. vegetable oil, plus more for frying
4 canned chipotle chiles en adobo
4 tbsp. roughly chopped cilantro
1 1/2 tbsp. sesame seeds, toasted
1/4 tsp. dried oregano
10 (6") corn tortillas, stacked and cut into 1 1/2" squares
6 oz. fresh chorizo, removed from casing and chopped into chunks
1/4 cup sour cream, to garnish
2 oz. cotija or feta cheese, crumbled, for garnish
4 radishes, thinly sliced
Kosher salt, to taste

Instructions

1. Heat oven to broil and place rack 6" from heating element. In a medium bowl, toss tomatoes, garlic, jalapeño, and onions with 2 tbsp. vegetable oil. Transfer ingredients to a foil-lined 9" x 13" baking pan and broil, turning occasionally as tomato skins start to blister and blacken, about 10 minutes. Transfer roasted vegetables to a food processor. Add chipotle chiles, 2 tbsp. cilantro, sesame seeds, oregano, and 1/4 cup water to the food processor and purée until smooth, about 1 minute. Set sauce aside.

2. Pour vegetable oil into a deep 12" cast-iron skillet until it reaches a depth of 1"; heat over medium-high heat until a deep-fry thermometer registers 350°. Working in 2 batches, add tortillas and fry, stirring occasionally, until golden brown and crisp, about 3 minutes per batch. Using a slotted spoon, transfer tortilla chips to a paper towel-lined baking sheet. Lightly season them with salt. Repeat with remaining tortillas. Set aside.

3. Heat a deep 12" nonstick skillet over medium-high heat. Add chorizo and cook, stirring frequently and breaking meat up into small pieces with a wooden spoon until browned and cooked through, 8–10 minutes. Add tomato-chipotle sauce to skillet, stir to combine, and season with salt. Bring to a simmer, add tortilla chips, and stir to combine. Let ingredients simmer until the tortilla chips just soften, about 2 minutes.

4. Transfer chilaquiles to a platter and garnish with remaining cilantro, sour cream, cheese, and radishes.

Mexican Scrambled Eggs

Yield: serves 4-6
Ingredients
3 tbsp. canola oil
1 small white onion, finely chopped
1 jalapeño, stemmed, seeded, and finely chopped
1 plum tomato, cored, seeded, and finely chopped
2 tbsp. thinly sliced cilantro leaves
Kosher salt and freshly ground black pepper, to taste
8 eggs, lightly beaten
Instructions
1.   Heat oil in a 12-inch skillet over medium-high heat. Add onion, jalapeño, and tomato, season with salt and pepper, and cook, stirring, until soft, about 6 minutes.
2.   Add cilantro and eggs, and cook, folding eggs over in large curds occasionally, until cooked through, about 4 minutes.

Some Random Pics...

Guisada al Pollo
Chicken and Potato Stew

Ingredients

1/4 cup canola oil

1 1/2 lb. boneless, skinless chicken thighs

Kosher salt and freshly ground black pepper, to taste

1 small white onion, chopped

1 medium carrot, chopped

1 red bell pepper, stemmed, seeded, and finely chopped

1 cup finely chopped fresh or canned pineapple

1 tsp. ground cumin

1 tsp. dried thyme

6 cloves garlic, minced

2 canned chipotles in adobo sauce, finely chopped

1 jalapeño, quartered lengthwise

1 lb. Yukon gold potatoes, peeled, cut into 1/2" cubes

4 cups chicken stock

3 sprigs epazote or cilantro

1 (15-oz.) can whole peeled tomatoes in juice, crushed

3 tbsp. capers, rinsed

Juice of 1 lime

Instructions

1.   Heat oil in a 6-qt. saucepan over medium-high heat. Season chicken with salt and pepper, and working in batches, add to pan, and cook, turning once, until browned on both sides and cooked through, about 15 minutes. Transfer to a plate and let cool; using a fork, finely shred meat and set aside.

2.   Return saucepan to heat, and add onion, carrot, and peppers; cook, stirring, until soft, about 8 minutes. Add pineapple, cumin, thyme, garlic, chipotles, and jalapeño, and cook, stirring, until fragrant, about 2 minutes. Add reserved shredded chicken back to pan along with potatoes, stock, epazote, and tomatoes, and bring to a boil; reduce heat to medium-low, and cook, stirring occasionally, until potatoes are tender, about 30 minutes. Add capers and juice, and season with salt and pepper before serving.

Sopa de Poro y Papa
Grilled Mexican Potato and Leek Soup

Yield: serves 8-10
Ingredients
4 tbsp. unsalted butter
3 medium leeks, white and light green parts only, roughly
chopped
2 medium white onions, roughly chopped
1 medium russet potato, peeled and roughly chopped
8 cups chicken stock
1 dried bay leaf
Kosher salt and freshly ground black pepper, to taste
1/2 cup crema or sour cream
2 tbsp. finely chopped chives
Olive oil, for garnish
Instructions
1.   Heat butter in a 4-qt. saucepan over medium heat. Add
leeks, onions, and potato, and cook, stirring often, until soft,
about 20 minutes. Add stock and bay leaf, and cook, stirring
occasionally, until potato is very tender, about 35 minutes.
Transfer to a blender and purée until smooth, at least 2 minutes;
season with salt and pepper. Transfer to a pitcher or bowl and
refrigerate until chilled, about 2 hours.
2.   To serve, divide chilled soup among serving bowls and
dollop with a spoonful of crema, sprinkle with some of the
chives, and drizzle with a couple drops of olive oil.

Red Chile Enchiladas

Ingredients

20 dried new mexico chiles
3 tbsp. canola oil, plus more for frying
10 cloves garlic
1/4 cup fresh lime juice
1 tbsp. ground cumin
2 tsp. sugar
Kosher salt, to taste
12 corn tortillas
2 cups grated mozzarella
2 cups grated sharp cheddar
3/4 cup finely chopped red onion
1/4 cup finely crumbled cotija cheese
3 tbsp. crema or sour cream

Instructions

1. Soften chiles. Transfer chiles and 2 cups soaking water to a food processor; let cool.

2. Heat oven to 450°. Heat oil in a 12" skillet over medium heat. Add garlic; cook until golden brown, about 2 minutes. Using a slotted spoon, transfer garlic to the food processor with the reserved chiles, reserving oil in skillet. Purée chile–garlic mixture; add lime, cumin, sugar, and salt and pulse to combine. Strain through a sieve; discard solids. Transfer chile sauce to reserved skillet; heat sauce over medium heat.

3. Pour oil into a 10" skillet over medium-high heat to a depth of 1/2". Using tongs and working with one tortilla at a time, dip tortilla in oil; cook until slightly crisp, about 15 seconds. Drain tortilla. Dip in chile sauce to coat, and transfer to a plate. Sprinkle some of the mozzarella, cheddar, and onions along center of tortilla. Roll up enchilada. Arrange rolled enchiladas on a baking sheet; bake until cheese is melted, about 5 minutes. Divide enchiladas between 4 plates; sprinkle with cotija cheese and drizzle with crema.

Blue Corn Pellizcadas
Salsa and Queso Fresco

Ingredients

2 cups prepared blue corn masa
1 cup Charred Tomato and Chile Salsa, or use store-
bought
1/2 cup (4 oz.) crumbled queso fresco Coarsely torn fresh
chipilín, cilantro, watercress, or radish leaves, for serving
Lime wedges, for serving

Instructions

1.   Divide the masa into 8 equal balls (about 2 ounces
each). Using your hands, press and shape each into a 4-
inch-wide round about twice the thickness of a tortilla.
2.   Using a wide spatula, lift the tortillas out of the pan
and flip them over onto the plate so the toasted side is
facing up. Pinch the tortillas all around the edges to form
a ridge like a pie crust; pinch some small ridges atop the
center of the masa as well to form little ponds to hold
the salsa. Fill each pellizcada with 2 tablespoons of salsa,
then sprinkle each evenly with 1 tablespoon of queso
fresco.
3.   Return the pellizcadas to the griddle or pan in
batches to heat thoroughly and soften the cheese
slightly. Remove to a plate, finish each with some of the
coarsely torn greens and a squeeze of lime juice, and
serve immediately.

Tamales with Black Beans

Yield: makes 14
Time: 2 hours, 55 minutes
Ingredients

1 package frozen banana leaves, thawed, center seams removed, leaves cut into 8-inch squares, scraps reserved

4 cups prepared blue corn masa

1/2 cup vegetable oil or lard

1 tbsp. plus 2 tsp. kosher salt

1 lb. cooked black beans, drained and rinsed (2½ cups)

Charred Tomato and Chile Salsa

Instructions

1.   Place the banana leaves in a wide bowl or baking dish of cold water while you prepare the masa. In a large bowl, combine the masa, lard or oil, and salt with your hands, kneading and squeezing the mixture until it forms a thick and pliable paste that doesn't crack around the edges. Cover and set aside for 30 minutes.

2.   Line the bottom of a medium pot with a few layers of banana leaves to keep the tamales from sticking (this is a good use for the scraps left over from cutting the squares). Add enough water to come about 3 inches up the sides of the pot. Cover the pot and set over low heat to warm.

3.   Turn the masa out onto a work surface. Flatten it into a large rectangle, and sprinkle the beans over the surface. Use the heels of your hands to press and knead the masa and beans together until they are well combined. Divide the mixture into fourteen ½ cup portions, then shape each into a chunky patty about ¾ inch thick. Wrap each patty loosely in a banana leaf square to cover, then stack the tamales seam side down in the pot. Cover the pot and adjust the heat as needed; steam until the masa is set, about 1 hour 10 minutes. Turn off the heat and let rest, covered, for 30 minutes. Serve warm with salsa.

Mexican Chicken and Vegetable Soup

Yield: serves 8-10
Time: 2 hours, 30 minutes
Ingredients
1 large farm-raised chicken, with skin (about 5 lb.), cut into serving-size pieces
4 chayotes (3 lb.), cut into 1½-inch wedges
8 medium carrots (1 lb. 4 oz.), peeled and cut into 1-inch chunks
8 small red potatoes (8 oz.), quartered
2 medium yellow onions (1 lb.), peeled and sliced
4 medium ripe tomatoes (2 lb.), skinned, seeded, and coarsely chopped
10 oz. green beans, trimmed (2 cups)
1/4 cup kosher salt, plus more to taste
1 large poblano pepper (4 oz.), stemmed, seeded, and cut in 1-inch strips
Fresh cilantro, for serving
Lime wedges, for serving
Corn tortillas, warmed, for serving
Instructions
1.   In a very large pot, add the chicken pieces (including the bones, feet, skin, and organs) and 6 quarts cold water. Bring to a low boil over high heat, and let cook for 20 minutes. Add the chayote, carrots, potatoes, and onions, and return the soup to a boil. Add the tomatoes, green beans, salt, and the poblano, return to a boil and cook until the vegetables are soft, the chicken is very tender, and the broth is flavorful, 60-70 minutes. Taste and adjust the seasoning as needed.
2.   Divide the chicken and some vegetables and broth among 8-10 large soup bowls. Top with fresh cilantro and serve hot with lime wedges and warm corn tortillas.

Some Random Pics...

Pescado Embarazado
Grilled Fish Skewers

Yield: serves 4
Time: 50 minutes
Ingredients
1¾ cups freshly squeezed orange juice
1¼ cups canned tomato purée
½ cup achiote paste
4 medium garlic cloves, finely chopped (2 Tbsp.)
2 tsp. cumin seeds
1½ tsp. finely chopped flat-leaf parsley
1½ tsp. finely chopped fresh rosemary
1½ tsp. finely chopped fresh thyme
Kosher salt
Freshly ground black pepper
Four 1-lb. whole mackerel or branzino, gutted and cleaned
(or substitute 2½ lb. dogfish or mahi mahi fillets, cut into
2-inch cubes)
Canola oil, for the grill
Salsa Huichol and lime wedges, for serving

Instructions

1.   Make the marinade: In a blender, add the orange juice, tomato purée, achiote paste, garlic, cumin, parsley, rosemary, and thyme. Blend until completely smooth, then transfer to a small pot.

2.   Bring to a boil over medium-high, then lower the heat to maintain a strong simmer. Cook, stirring occasionally to prevent scorching, until the marinade is slightly thickened and the garlic no longer tastes raw, 15–20 minutes. Season with salt and pepper to taste, then transfer to a heatproof bowl and let cool to room temperature. Use immediately, or refrigerate, covered, for up to 1 week.

3.   If using whole fish, use a sharp knife to score the fish crosswise on each side, being careful not to cut through to the bone. Rub 1½ cups of the marinade all over the outside of the fish and inside the slits. (If using cubes, toss the fish with 1½ cups of the marinade in a large bowl.) Let marinate at room temperature while you preheat the grill, at least 15 and up to 40 minutes.

4.   Preheat a grill over medium-high heat, or a grill pan or griddle over high heat. When the grill is hot, liberally oil the grates. Thread the fish onto 4 metal or bamboo skewers. Grill, turning occasionally, until the fish is charred in places and cooked through, 14–16 minutes for whole fish, 5–6 minutes for cubed fish. Transfer to a platter and serve with lime wedges, Salsa Huichol, and the remaining marinade.

Palanquetas de Cacahuates Mexican Peanut Brittle

Yield: makes One 9-Inch Square
Time: 30 minutes
Ingredients

Butter, for greasing

1/2 cup sugar

2 tbsp. piloncillo

2 tbsp. honey

1/4 tsp. kosher salt

2 tbsp. unsalted butter, cut into small pieces

2 cups toasted peanuts

Instructions

1. Lightly grease a 9-inch square baking dish with butter; set aside.

2. In a small pot, add the sugar, piloncillo, honey, salt, and ¼ cup water; swirl with your fingers to combine. Using clean, wet fingers, brush away any sugar remaining along the sides of the pan. Set over medium-high heat and bring to a boil; cook without stirring until the syrup reaches a dark caramel stage on a candy thermometer, 345°–350°F, 18–22 minutes. Remove from the heat; quickly add the butter and peanuts, and stir with a wooden spoon until combined.

3. Scrape the mixture into the baking dish; use the spoon or your hands to press the candy into an even layer. While the candy is still pliable, overturn it onto a cutting board and slice into squares or bars. Let cool completely and serve, or transfer to an airtight container and store for up to 1 week at room temperature.

Salsa de Cacahuate y Chile de Arbol

Yield: makes About 1 Cup
Ingredients
2 tbsp. olive oil
1/4 cup roasted unsalted peanuts
1/4 tsp. dried thyme
6 dried arbol chiles, stemmed
8 black peppercorns
6 allspice berries
4 cloves garlic, minced
1 small white onion, minced
1 tsp. apple cider vinegar
1 tsp. kosher salt
Instructions
1.   Heat oil in an 8″ skillet over medium heat; add peanuts, thyme, chiles, peppercorns, allspice, garlic, and onion, and cook, stirring, until onion is soft, about 4 minutes. Transfer to a blender and add vinegar, salt and 1/2 cup water; blend until very smooth, about 2 minutes. Let cool.

Tacos de Papa

Ingredients
1 tbsp. finely chopped cilantro
1/2 tsp. dried oregano
1/2 tsp. sugar
2 ripe tomatoes, cored
2 red jalapeños, stemmed
1 clove garlic, smashed, plus 2 cloves, minced
1 tbsp. unsalted butter
1 lb. russet potatoes, peeled
2 tsp. kosher salt
1 tsp. freshly ground black pepper, plus more to taste
1 tsp. ground cumin
1/2 cup canola oil
18 corn tortillas
Thinly sliced green cabbage and tomatoes, and crumbled cotija cheese, for serving

Instructions

1.   Puree cilantro, oregano, sugar, tomatoes, jalapeños, smashed garlic, and 2/3 cup water in a blender until smooth; set salsa aside. Bring a medium saucepan of salted water to a boil, add potatoes, and cook until tender, about 25 minutes. Drain potatoes and transfer to a large bowl. Add minced garlic, butter, salt, pepper, and cumin, and mash until smooth. Set potato mixture aside.

2.   Heat oil in a 12″ skillet over medium-high heat. Spread 1 heaping tbsp. potato mixture over half of each tortilla, and fold over to form a taco. Working in batches, add tacos to oil and fry, turning once, until golden brown and crisp, about 3 minutes.

3.   Stuff cabbage, tomatoes, and cotija into tacos; drizzle with salsa before serving.

Some Random Pics...

Mole Verde Zascatecano

Yield: serves 6

For the Chicken

1 (3–4-lb.) whole chicken, cut into 8 pieces

1/2 cup chopped cilantro stems

2 tbsp. kosher salt

1 tsp. whole black peppercorns

2 cloves garlic

1 large yellow onion, chopped

1 bay leaf

For the Mole Verde

8 oz. tomatillos, peeled and chopped

2 jalapeños, stemmed and chopped

1/2 cup cilantro leaves

2 tsp. kosher salt, plus more to taste

2 cloves garlic, chopped

2 (8-inch) flour tortillas, toasted, plus more for serving

3 tbsp. canola oil

Mexican rice, for serving

Instructions

1. Cook the chicken: Place chicken, cilantro, salt, peppercorns, garlic, onion, bay leaf, and 12 cups water in a 6-qt. saucepan and bring to a boil; reduce heat to medium-low and cook, covered and stirring occasionally, until chicken is tender, about 30 minutes.

2. Remove chicken from saucepan and strain liquid through a fine strainer; reserve 4 cups, and save remaining liquid for another use. Set chicken and liquid aside.

3. Heat tomatillos and jalapeños in a 4-qt. saucepan over medium heat and cook, stirring occasionally, until darkened and thick, about 10 minutes. Transfer to a blender with cilantro, salt, garlic, tortillas, and 1 cup reserved cooking liquid; puree.

4. Heat oil in a 6-qt. saucepan over medium-high heat; add tomatillo sauce and fry, stirring constantly, until it thickens into a paste, about 5 minutes. Whisk in remaining cooking liquid and bring to a boil; reduce heat to medium-low and cook, stirring, until reduced and thickened, about 30 minutes.

5. Add chicken pieces and cook until heated through, about 10 minutes. Serve with Mexican rice and tortillas.

Guiso de Flor de Calabaza
Squash Blossom Saute

Yield: serves 4

Ingredients

1 tbsp. canola oil
1/4 small yellow onion, minced
1 clove garlic, minced
1/2 red jalapeño, stemmed, seeded, minced
2 calabazitas (Mexican squash), summer squash, or zucchini, halved, seeded, thinly sliced crosswise
1 ripe tomato, cored, minced
1 tbsp. minced fresh epazote
20 squash blossoms, stemmed (both the epazote and blossoms are available from Melissas.com)
Kosher salt and freshly ground black pepper, to taste

Instructions

1. Heat oil in a 12″ skillet over medium-high heat. Add onion and cook, stirring, until soft, about 2 minutes. Add garlic and jalapeño and cook, stirring, until fragrant, about 1 minute. Add squash and cook, covered and stirring occasionally, until tender, about 3 minutes. Add tomato, and cook, stirring, for 5 minutes. Remove skillet from heat, and stir in epazote, squash blossoms, salt, and pepper; let cool for 5 minutes before serving.

Rebocado
Pork Neck and Purslane Stew

Yield: serves 6-8

Ingredients

2 tbsp. kosher salt, plus more to taste

1/2 tsp. cumin seeds

14 dried New Mexico chiles, stemmed

1 whole clove

1 bay leaf

1/2 stick cinnamon

2 lb. pork neck, cut into ¾″-thick slices by butcher

3 lb. purslane leaves and small stems

Warm flour tortillas, for serving

Instructions

1. Place salt, cumin, chiles, clove, bay leaf, cinnamon, and 2½ cups boiling water in a blender, and puree until smooth. Transfer to a 6-qt. saucepan with pork and 4 cups water, bring to a boil, reduce heat to medium-low, and cook, covered and stirring occasionally, until meat is tender, about 2 hours.

2. Add purslane and cook, stirring occasionally, until tender, about another 30 minutes.

3. Divide pork and purslane among serving bowls, ladle sauce over top, and serve with tortillas.

Sopa de Habas
Fava Bean Soup

Yield: serves 4

Ingredients

2 cups shelled, dried fava beans

1 ripe tomato, chopped

1 clove garlic, chopped

1/2 small yellow onion, chopped

Kosher salt and freshly ground black pepper, to taste

1 tbsp. olive oil

1/4 tsp. crushed saffron threads

1/4 tsp. ground cumin

Instructions

1.   Bring fava beans and 4 cups water to a boil in a 4-qt. saucepan over high heat; reduce heat to medium-low and cook, covered and stirring, until tender, about 40 minutes.

2.   Meanwhile, make the recado: Combine tomato, garlic, onion, salt, and pepper in a blender or food processor and puree; set aside.

3.   Heat oil in another 4-qt. saucepan over medium-high heat. Add recado and cook, stirring constantly, until it begins to thicken, about 5 minutes.

4.   Add the fava beans along with their cooking liquid, saffron, and cumin. Cook the beans, stirring occasionally, until flavors meld and beans are very tender and break up in the soup, about 10 minutes.

Roasted Tomatillo Salsa Chipotle and Roasted Garlic

Yield: makes 1 1/4 CUPS
Ingredients
8 oz. tomatillos, husked and rinsed
6 cloves garlic, peeled
3 dried chipotle chiles, stemmed
1/2 tsp. kosher salt
Instructions
1.　Heat oven to 500°. Place tomatillos on a foil-lined baking sheet and roast, turning halfway through cooking, until blackened in spots and cooked through, about 20 minutes; let cool.
2.　Meanwhile, heat a 12″ cast-iron skillet over medium-low heat; add garlic and chiles, and toast, turning, until chiles and garlic are blistered and blackened in spots, about 10 minutes. Transfer to a blender along with tomatillos, salt, and 1/2 cup water; blend until smooth. Let cool.

Salsa de Tomatillo y Pina

Yield: makes About 3 1/4 Cups
Ingredients
1 lb. tomatillos, husked and rinsed
3 jalapeños, stemmed
4 tbsp. unsalted butter
1 lb. chopped fresh pineapple
1 tsp. cumin seeds
1 stick Mexican cinnamon, crushed
1 tart apple, peeled, cored, and roughly chopped
2 cloves garlic, peeled
2 tbsp. olive oil
1/4 cup passion fruit juice
1 tbsp. apple cider vinegar
1 tbsp. sugar
Kosher salt, to taste

Instructions

1.   Bring a 4-qt. saucepan of water to a boil and add tomatillos and jalapeños; cook until tender, about 10 minutes. Drain and set aside.

2.   Heat butter in a 12″ skillet over high heat; add pineapple, cumin, cinnamon, and apple, and cook, stirring constantly, until beginning to caramelize, about 5 minutes. Reduce heat to medium-low, and cook, stirring, until fruit is tender, about 20 minutes. Transfer to a food processor along with ½ cup water and puree until very smooth; pour purée through a fine strainer into a bowl and discard solids. Return purée to food processor and add boiled tomatillos and jalapeños along with garlic, and pulse until slightly chunky.

3.   Heat oil in a 6-qt. saucepan over high heat; add salsa and ½ cup water and bring to a boil. Reduce heat to low and cook, stirring, until thickened, about 45 minutes. Add passion fruit juice, vinegar, and sugar, and cook for 1 minute. Remove from heat and let cool.

Escabeche de Cebolla Yucatecan Pickled Red Onions

Yield: makes About 1 3/4 Cups
Ingredients
1 tbsp. kosher salt
1 large red onion, thinly sliced lengthwise
1 tsp. whole black peppercorns
1 tsp. dried oregano
1 tsp. cumin seeds
3 cloves garlic, peeled and halved lengthwise
1 1/2 cups red wine vinegar
Instructions
1.   In a bowl, toss salt and onion together; let sit until onion releases some of its liquid, about 15 minutes. Transfer to jar along with peppercorns, oregano, cumin, and garlic, and pour over vinegar; seal with lid. Refrigerate at least 4 hours before using.

Salsa de Pina Picante

Yield: makes About 1 1/3 Cups
Ingredients
1 cup finely chopped fresh pineapple
1/4 cup finely chopped cilantro
3 tbsp. fresh lime juice
2 tbsp. fresh orange juice
1 1/2 tsp. sugar
1 tsp. kosher salt
2 jalapeños, stemmed and minced
1/2 small red onion, minced
Instructions
1. In a large bowl, mix together all ingredients; serve at room temperature.

Salsa de Tomatillo en Molacajete Roasted Tomatillo and Serrano Salsa

Yield: makes About 1 Cup
Ingredients
1 lb. tomatillos, husked and rinsed
4 serrano chiles, stemmed
3 cloves garlic, peeled
1 tsp. kosher salt
1/4 cup finely chopped cilantro
2 tbsp. minced white onion
2 1/2 tsp. fresh lime juice
1 tbsp. olive oil
Instructions
1.   Position an oven rack 4" from broiler; heat to high. Place tomatillos, chiles, and garlic on a foil-lined baking sheet and broil, turning often, until blackened in spots and cooked through, about 10 minutes for the garlic and chiles, and 15 minutes for the tomatillos; remove each ingredient as it finishes cooking.
2.   Place roasted chiles, garlic, and salt in a food processor and puree until smooth; add tomatillos, cilantro, onion, and lime juice. Pulse until roughly chopped. Transfer to a bowl and stir in oil.

Salsa Playera de Lujo
Fresh Tomato and Olive Salsa

Yield: makes About 2 Cups
Ingredients

1 lb. ripe tomatoes, cored, seeded, and finely chopped
¼ cups finely chopped cilantro
2 tbsp. finely chopped pitted green olives
1 tbsp. finely chopped pickled jalapeños, plus 1½ tsp. liquid from jar
1 tbsp. capers, rinsed
1½ tsp. ketchup
1½ tsp. olive oil
1½ tsp. kosher salt
½ small white onion, minced

Instructions

1. In a large bowl, toss together all ingredients; let sit for 30 minutes to blend flavors. Serve at room temperature or chilled.

Gorditas de Huevos
Masa Cakes Stuffed With Eggs

Yield: serves 6
Ingredients
2 cups masa harina
1 tsp. kosher salt, plus more to taste
2 dried New Mexico chiles, stemmed and seeded
2 cloves garlic
6 eggs, lightly beaten
Instructions
1.   In a medium bowl, stir together masa harina, salt, and 1 1/4 cups water until dough forms; let sit for 5 minutes. Divide into six 2″ balls (about 3 oz. each), then flatten with your hands into 1/4″-thick disks. Set aside.
2.   Heat chiles in a 10″ skillet over high heat and cook, turning, until lightly toasted, about 3 minutes; reduce heat to medium. Transfer chiles to a blender, add garlic and 1/2 cup water, and puree; return to skillet; add eggs and cook, stirring often, until cooked through, about 8 minutes. Set aside.
3.   Heat a 12″ cast-iron skillet over medium-high heat. Working in batches, add disks, season with salt, and cook, turning once, until golden brown on both sides, about 4 minutes. Immediately transfer to a work surface, cut horizontally halfway through disk, and stuff with scrambled egg mixture. Serve immediately.

Gorditas Zacatecanas
Zacatecan Baked Masa Cakes

Yield: serves 8
For the Bean Filling
2 dried New Mexico chiles, stemmed and seeded
3/4 tsp. ground cumin
1 clove garlic
1 tbsp. canola oil
2 cups cooked pinto beans
Kosher salt and freshly ground black pepper, to taste
For the Gorditas
2 cups masa harina
1 tsp. kosher salt
1/2 cup vegetable shortening
Instructions

1.   Make the bean filling: Heat chiles in a 10″ skillet over high heat and cook, turning, until lightly toasted, about 5 minutes. Transfer to a blender with cumin, garlic, and 1/2 cup water; puree until smooth. Heat oil in a skillet over medium heat and add chile mixture, beans, salt, and pepper; mash with a fork and cook, stirring often, until thickened but not dry, about 20 minutes. Set aside.

2.   Make the gorditas: Heat oven to 400°. In a large bowl, whisk together masa harina and salt; add shortening and 1 1/4 cups water, and stir until dough forms. Divide into eight 2″ balls (about 2 1/2 oz. each); flatten each into a 1/4″-thick disk, and place 1 heaping tbsp. bean filling in center. Wrap disk around filling, pinching edges together to seal, then transfer, seam side down, to a parchment paper–lined baking sheet. Bake until golden brown, about 30 minutes.

Frijoles de la Olla
Stewed Beans with Pico de Gallo

Yield: serves 6-8
Ingredients
2 cups dried pinto beans
1 clove garlic, smashed
1 whole jalapeño, plus 1/2 stemmed, seeded, minced
1/2 small yellow onion, plus 1/4 minced
Kosher salt and freshly ground black pepper, to taste
1/4 cup minced cilantro
1 tomato, cored, seeded, and finely chopped
Crumbled cotija cheese and flour tortillas, for serving

Instructions Bring beans, garlic, whole jalapeño, 1/2 whole onion, and 8 cups water to a boil in a 4-qt. saucepan over high heat; reduce heat to medium-low, season with salt and pepper, and cook, covered and stirring occasionally, until beans are just tender, about 1 hour 45 minutes. Meanwhile, make pico de gallo by stirring remaining jalapeño and onion with cilantro and tomato in a small bowl until combined. Ladle beans into serving bowls, and top with pico de gallo and cotija. Serve with warm tortillas

Shredded Beef
Lime and Avocado

Yield: serves 12
Ingredients
2 lb. flat-cut beef brisket, trimmed
2 cloves garlic, smashed
2 bay leaves
1 large onion, sliced
1/4 lb. jack cheese, cubed
1/4 cup fresh lime juice
1/4 cup finely chopped cilantro
1 tbsp. chopped canned chipotle chiles en adobo
4 scallions, chopped
3 medium tomatoes, cored, seeded, and finely chopped
Warmed corn tortillas, for serving
1 avocado, pitted and sliced
Sweet paprika, to taste
Kosher salt and freshly ground black pepper, to taste

Instructions
1.   Bring the beef, garlic, bay leaves, onions, salt, and 6 cups water to a boil in a 6-qt. dutch oven. Reduce heat to low, cover, and simmer until the brisket is tender, about 3 hours.
2.   Remove pot from heat and let brisket cool, uncovered. Transfer brisket to a cutting board; shred with your fingers. Roughly chop meat; transfer to a bowl. Mix in the cheese, lime juice, cilantro, chipotles, scallions, and tomatoes. Season with salt and pepper. Serve the salpicón wrapped in tortillas and topped with paprika and avocado slices.

Chile-Rubbed Roast Turkey

Yield: serves 12
Ingredients
6 pasilla chiles, stemmed and seeded
30 cloves garlic (5 finely chopped)
1/3 cup orange juice
3 tbsp. extra-virgin olive oil
2 tbsp. honey
1 tbsp. kosher salt, plus more to taste
1 tbsp. whole black peppercorns
1 (12-lb.) turkey
1 large onion, quartered
1 orange, quartered
1/2 cup port or red wine
2 tbsp. unsalted butter
4 cups turkey or chicken broth
1 1/2 tbsp. cornstarch mixed with 3 tbsp. water
1/2 tsp. freshly grated nutmeg
2 tbsp. finely chopped flat-leaf parsley

Instructions

1. In a 10" cast-iron skillet over high heat, toast chiles, turning once, until fragrant, about 2 minutes. Transfer to a small bowl and cover with 1 cup boiling water; let soak until soft, 20 minutes. Transfer chiles and their liquid to a blender along with 25 cloves garlic, orange juice, oil, honey, 1 tbsp. salt, and peppercorns and purée until smooth, about 2 minutes. Set chile rub aside.

2. Heat oven to 500° and place rack in bottom third of oven. Season inside of turkey with salt. Rub turkey with chile rub and stuff with onions and oranges; transfer turkey breast side up to a rack set in a roasting pan. Roast for 30 minutes; lower heat to 325° and cook for 30 minutes more. Remove turkey from oven and, using kitchen towels to protect your hands, flip turkey breast side down. Roast, basting occasionally, until an instant-read thermometer inserted into a thigh but not touching the bone registers 165°, about 3 hours total for a 12-lb. turkey. Lower oven to 150°. Transfer turkey, breast side up, to a baking sheet; return to oven to keep warm. Remove turkey from oven 15 minutes before serving.

3. Meanwhile, add port to roasting pan and heat over high heat. Scrape up any brown bits; cook, stirring, until mixture has reduced by half, about 5 minutes. Set a sieve over a bowl; strain liquid and discard solids. Put liquid into freezer and leave for 30 minutes. Skim and discard fat; set liquid aside. Melt butter in a 12" skillet over medium-high heat. Add remaining garlic; cook until soft, about 2 minutes. Add broth and reserved liquid; boil to reduce by half, about 15 minutes. Whisk in cornstarch mixture; boil; strain through a sieve into a 1-qt. saucepan. Stir in nutmeg and parsley; season gravy with salt and pepper. Carve turkey and serve with the gravy.

Mexican Rice Pilaf

Yield: serves 8
Ingredients
2 tbsp. unsalted butter
5 ribs celery, chopped
2 medium white onions, chopped
1 red bell pepper, chopped
6 cloves garlic, chopped
2 poblano chiles, roasted, peeled, stemmed, seeded, and
chopped
2 tsp. ground cumin seeds
1 tsp. freshly ground black pepper
3 bay leaves
1 chile de árbol
2 cups long-grain white rice
2 1/2 cups chicken broth
1/4 cup cilantro, finely chopped
Kosher salt, to taste
1/4 cup parsley, finely chopped

Instructions

1.   Melt the butter in a 6-qt. Dutch oven over medium-high heat. Add the celery, onions, and bell pepper and cook, stirring occasionally, until soft, about 10 minutes. Add the garlic, chiles, cumin, pepper, bay leaves, and chile de árbol and cook, stirring occasionally, until soft and fragrant, 3–4 minutes.

2.   Add the rice and broth, season with salt, and bring to a boil. Reduce heat to low, cover, and simmer until the rice is tender, about 30 minutes. Remove pot from heat and let sit, covered, for 10 minutes. Add cilantro and parsley and fluff rice with a fork before serving.

Creamed Roasted Onions

Yield: serves 8

Ingredients

3 lb. pearl onions, trimmed and peeled

2 cups chicken broth

1 1/2 cups half-and-half

3 tbsp. unsalted butter

4 cloves garlic, finely chopped

3 tbsp. flour

2 cups corn kernels, fresh or frozen and thawed

2 tbsp. finely chopped parsley

2 tbsp. Worcestershire

1 tbsp. brandy or port

1 tsp. ground cumin

1/2 tsp. ancho chile powder or other chile powder

1/2 tsp. freshly grated nutmeg

Mexican hot sauce, such as Cholula, to taste

Sea salt and freshly ground black pepper, to taste

Instructions

1. Heat oven to broil and place a rack 4" from heating element. Put onions on a rimmed baking sheet and broil, turning occasionally with tongs, until slightly charred, about 12 minutes; set aside on a rack to let cool.

2. In a 2-qt. saucepan, bring the chicken broth and half-and-half to a gentle boil; remove from heat and set aside. Meanwhile, melt the butter in a 4-qt. saucepan over medium heat. Add the garlic and cook, stirring occasionally, until soft, about 2 minutes. Add the flour and whisk until golden, about 1 minute. Slowly whisk in the reserved chicken broth mixture. Add the corn, parsley, Worcestershire, port, cumin, chile powder, nutmeg, and hot sauce. Reduce heat to medium and cook, stirring occasionally, until thick and creamy, about 15 minutes. Add the reserved onions, season with salt and pepper, and cook until the flavors meld.

Fish Tacos

Yield: serves 4
Ingredients
1 1/2 cups shredded green cabbage
2 limes (1 cut into wedges)
1 1/2 tbsp. kosher salt, plus more to taste
2 cups flour
1/2 cup cornstarch
1 (12-oz.) bottle dark beer
1 egg
Canola oil, for frying
1 lb. boneless, skinless red snapper, cut into 1½" strips
2 tsp. chili powder
16 corn tortillas
1/4 red onion, thinly sliced
4 sprigs cilantro, chopped
1 tomato, cored and chopped
Sour cream or crema
Mexican hot sauce

Instructions

1.   In a bowl, combine cabbage and juice of 1 lime; season with salt, to taste; chill. In another bowl, whisk together 1½ tbsp. salt, 1½ cups flour, cornstarch, beer, and egg to make a batter.

2.   Pour oil into a 5-qt. Dutch oven to a depth of 2"; heat until a thermometer reads 375°. Sprinkle fish with chili powder and salt. Put remaining flour on a plate. Dredge fish in flour; shake off excess. Working in batches, dip fish in batter and fry until crisp, about 3 minutes. Transfer to a rack set inside keep warm in 200° oven.

3.   Heat a skillet over medium-high heat. Working in batches, add tortillas; cook, flipping, until warmed. To serve, layer 2 tortillas together, fill with some of the fish and cabbage, squeeze with a lime wedge, and garnish with onion, cilantro, tomato, sour cream, and hot sauce. Repeat.

Huevos Rancheros

Yield: serves 4
Ingredients
14 plum tomatoes, cored
12 tbsp. canola oil
3 cloves garlic, minced
1/2 jalapeño, stemmed and minced
1/2 medium yellow onion, chopped
1 tbsp. fresh lime juice
Kosher salt and freshly ground black pepper, to taste
8 corn tortillas
8 eggs
Pickled jalapeño slices, for garnish
Instructions
1.   Heat a 12" cast-iron skillet over high heat. Add tomatoes; cook, turning, until skins blacken, 8–10 minutes. Peel tomatoes; purée in blender; strain; set aside.
2.   Heat 4 tbsp. oil in a 4-qt. pan over medium heat. Add garlic, jalapeños, and onions; cook until soft, 6–8 minutes. Add tomatoes; boil. Stir in lime juice; season with salt and pepper.
3.   Working in 4 batches, heat 1 tbsp. oil in a 12" nonstick skillet over medium-high heat; add 2 tortillas; cook, flipping once, until warmed, about 20 seconds. Transfer tortillas to 4 plates. Working in 2 batches, heat remaining oil in skillet over medium heat; cook eggs to desired doneness. Top each tortilla with a fried egg and tomato sauce. Garnish with pickled jalapeños.

Mexican Style Roasted Corn

Yield: serves 4

Ingredients

4 large ears corn, with husks still attached

1/2 cup mayonnaise

1 1/2 cups crumbled cotija cheese

4 tbsp. minced fresh cilantro

4 tsp. ancho chile powder

Kosher salt and freshly ground black pepper, to taste

1 lime, cut into four wedges

Instructions

1. Working with one ear of corn at a time, peel back the husks to expose the kernels, leaving husks attached at the base; remove the silk threads and tie husks together with kitchen twine around base of cob to form a handle. Repeat with remaining ears. Transfer corn to a large bowl or pot of water and let soak for 30 minutes.

2. Build a medium-hot fire in a charcoal grill or heat a gas grill over medium-high heat. Transfer corn to grill; cook, turning occasionally, until charred and cooked through, about 20 minutes. Remove corn from grill and brush with mayonnaise. Place cheese on a plate and roll each ear of corn in cheese to coat. Sprinkle corn evenly with some of the cilantro, chile powder, and salt and pepper, pressing the corn so that seasonings and cheese will adhere to the mayonnaise. Serve with lime wedges.

Refried Beans with Chorizo

Yield: serves 4-6
Ingredients
3 cups dried pinto beans, rinsed
Kosher salt, to taste
6 oz. fresh chorizo, casings removed
1 cup lard
Freshly ground black pepper, to taste
2 tbsp. minced cilantro
Instructions
1.　Put beans and 12 cups water into an 8-qt. pot; bring to a boil. Reduce heat to medium, season with salt; cook, adding more water if necessary, until beans are very tender, 2–2 1/2 hours. Drain beans, reserving 3 cups cooking liquid.
2.　Heat a 6-qt. pot over medium-high heat. Add chorizo and cook, breaking up into small pieces, until crisp, 6–8 minutes. Using a slotted spoon, remove half the chorizo; transfer to a plate and set aside. Add lard and let melt. Add beans; mash vigorously. Add 2 cups reserved cooking liquid; cook, stirring often, until hot, 3–5 minutes. (Stir in more liquid, if you like.) Season beans with salt and pepper and serve with reserved chorizo and cilantro.

Fish Tacos
Roasted Tomato Salsa

Yield: serves 4
Ingredients
2 cloves garlic, unpeeled
2 plum tomatoes
1 serrano chile
2 dried guajillo chiles or 1 ancho chile and 1 pasilla
chile
3 tbsp. chopped fresh cilantro
Kosher salt and sugar, to taste
1 cup cooked or canned pinto beans
16 (6") white corn tortillas
Canola oil, for frying
10 oz. boneless, skinless flounder or halibut filets,
cut into 3" x 1/2" strips
2 tsp. chili powder
1/2 cup flour
1 avocado, peeled, pitted, and thinly sliced
1 lime, cut into wedges Sour cream, for serving

Instructions

1.   Make the salsa: Heat a 12" cast-iron skillet over medium heat. Add garlic, tomatoes, and serrano chile and cook, turning occasionally, until charred all over. Transfer vegetables to a plate and let cool. Peel the garlic and stem and seed the serrano chile. Transfer vegetables and 2 tbsp. water to a small food processor and process into a chunky purée; set aside. Return skillet to medium-high heat. Add guajillo chiles and cook, flipping once, until toasted, 2 minutes. Transfer chiles to a bowl and cover with 2 cups hot water; let sit for 20 minutes to soften. Peel, stem, and seed chiles and purée; in food processor with tomato mixture. Add 1 tbsp. cilantro. Season salsa with salt and sugar, transfer to a bowl, cover, and set aside.

2.   Make the tacos: Put beans into a small pot and heat over medium heat until hot; cover, remove from heat, and keep warm. Heat a 12" skillet over medium-high heat. Working in batches, add tortillas and toast, turning occasionally, until soft, about 3 minutes. Stack tortillas on a sheet of aluminum foil and cover to keep warm. Pour oil into a 5-qt. pot to a depth of 2" and heat over medium-high heat until a deep-fry thermometer reads 350°. Meanwhile, season fish with salt and chili powder and dredge in flour, shaking off excess. Working in batches, add fish to the oil and cook, turning occasionally, until golden brown. Using a slotted spoon, transfer fish to a rack set in a baking sheet. To serve, use 2 tortillas per taco. Divide beans among tacos; top beans with fish, avocado, the remaining cilantro, a squeeze of lime juice, a dollop of sour cream, and a tablespoon of salsa. Serve warm.

Cemita Poblana
Puebla style Sandwich

Yield: serves 4
Ingredients
1 cup flour
4 eggs, beaten
1 cup bread crumbs
4 (1/4″) thick veal cutlets
Kosher salt and freshly ground black pepper, to taste
1/4 cup canola oil
4 round rolls, split and toasted
2 avocados, pitted, peeled, and thinly sliced
12 oz. queso blanco or mozzarella, grated
8 thin slices yellow onion
8 chipotle chiles in adobo, finely chopped, plus 3 tbsp. sauce
from the can
Instructions
1.　Place flour, eggs, and bread crumbs in three separate shallow dishes. Season veal with salt and pepper, and coat with flour, shaking off excess. Dip in eggs, then dredge in bread crumbs. Set aside.
2.　Heat oil in a 12″ skillet over medium-high heat, and cook veal cutlets, turning once, until golden brown on both sides, about 6 minutes. Using tongs, transfer to paper towels to drain.
3.　Place 1 veal cutlet on the bottom half of each roll and top with half an avocado, 3 oz. cheese, 2 slices onion, and 1/4 of the chipotle sauce. Cover with top bun.

Torta Ahogada
Mexican droned Sandwich

Yield: serves 1
Ingredients
3/4 oz. dried chiles de arbol (about 30), stemmed and seeded
3/4 cup cider vinegar
2 tbsp. pumpkin seeds, toasted
1 1/2 tbsp. sesame seeds, toasted
1 tsp. dried oregano
1 tsp. kosher salt
1/4 tsp. ground cumin
1/8 tsp. ground allspice
1/8 tsp. ground cloves
2 cloves garlic
1 crusty bolillo or Italian roll
1 1/2 cups leftover roasted pork shoulder, shredded
1/4 small yellow onion, thinly sliced
1 radish, thinly sliced
Instructions
1.   Combine chiles, vinegar, pumpkin and sesame seeds, oregano, salt, cumin, allspice, cloves, and garlic in a blender, and puree until very smooth. Pour through a medium strainer into a bowl, discard solids, and stir in 3/4 cup water.
2.   Heat oven to 350°. Split roll and fill bottom half with pork. Place on baking sheet and bake until warmed through and bread is toasted, about 6 minutes. Add onion, radish, and top bun; pour chile de arbol sauce over sandwich, and let sit, so that the sauce soaks in.

Pambazos
Salsa Dipped Potato and Chorizo Sandwiches

Yield: serves 6
Ingredients
15 dried guajillo chiles
1 clove garlic
1/2 small white onion, roughly chopped
2 1/4 lb. Yukon gold potatoes, peeled and cut into 1/2" cubes
Kosher salt, to taste
1/2 cup canola oil
1 1/4 lb. fresh chorizo, casings removed
6 soft pambazos, teleras or kaiser rolls, split
3 shredded iceberg lettuce
2 cups grated queso Oaxaca or mozzarella
3/4 cup crema or sour cream

Instructions

1. Heat a 12" skillet over medium-high heat. Working in batches, add chiles, and cook, turning once, until toasted, about 2 minutes. Transfer all chiles to a large bowl; pour over 4 cups boiling water, and let sit until chiles are soft, about 30 minutes. Drain, reserving 1 1/4 cups soaking liquid, and remove stems and seeds from chiles. Transfer chiles and reserved soaking liquid to a blender along with garlic and onion; purée until very smooth, at least 2 minutes. Pour sauce into a bowl; set aside.

2. Bring a 4-qt. saucepan of salted water to a boil over high heat; add potatoes, and cook until just tender, about 10 minutes. Drain and set aside. Heat 2 tbsp. oil in a 12" skillet over medium heat; add chorizo, and cook, stirring to break up into small pieces, until browned and cooked through, about 8 minutes. Add potatoes, and cook until potatoes are very tender, about 2 minutes; season with salt and pepper and set aside.

3. Using your fingers, scoop out and discard the insides of rolls, leaving a 1/2"-thick shell. Place about 1 cup potato-chorizo mixture on roll bottoms, and cover with tops; press sandwiches lightly to flatten and compact filling. Heat 2 tbsp. oil in a 12" skillet over medium-high heat. Submerge two sandwiches in chile sauce until thoroughly soaked, at least 10 seconds; place in skillet, and cook, pressing constantly with a metal spatula to flatten and flipping once, until browned on both sides, about 5 minutes. Transfer to a cutting board; repeat with remaining oil, sandwiches, and sauce. Open sandwiches and divide lettuce, cheese, and crema among sandwiches; close sandwiches again and serve warm.

Molletes
Mexican Bean and Cheese Sandwich

Yield: serves 8

For the Salsa

2 lb. plum tomatoes, cored, and cut into 1/2" cubes

2/3 cup roughly chopped cilantro

6 serrano chiles, stemmed, seeded, and finely chopped

1 large white onion, finely chopped

Kosher salt, to taste

For the Beans and Rolls

1/2 cup lard or canola oil

4 cloves garlic, minced

1 small white onion, finely chopped

2 cups chicken stock

3 (15-oz.) cans pinto beans, drained and rinsed

Kosher salt and freshly ground black pepper, to taste

4 bolillos or kaiser rolls, split

12 oz. queso Oaxaca, grated

Instructions

1.   To make the salsa, combine tomatoes, cilantro, chiles, and onion in a bowl, and season liberally with salt; fold gently to combine. Cover, and refrigerate, for about 1 hour.

2.   To make the refried beans, heat lard in a 12" skillet over medium-high heat. Add garlic and onion, and cook, stirring, until soft, about 8 minutes. Add stock and beans, and cook, stirring and mashing, until almost all beans are smooth and mixture is slightly soupy, about 5 minutes. Season with salt and pepper, and keep warm.

3.   Heat broiler to high. Using your fingers, scoop out and discard the insides of rolls, leaving a 1/2"-thick shell. Place roll halves on a foil-lined baking sheet with their cut sides up, and broil until lightly toasted, about 2 minutes. Pour about 1/2 cup refried beans over each roll half so that the beans are spilling over the edges, and then sprinkle with cheese. Return to broiler, and heat until beans are heated through and cheese is just melted, but not browned, about 2 minutes. Transfer one roll half to each serving plate, and top each with a couple large spoonfuls of salsa. Serve immediately.

Sopa de Lima
Lime Soup

Yield: serves 8-10
Ingredients
2 cups canola oil, for frying
12 corn tortillas, cut into 1/4" thick strips
4 cloves garlic, peeled
4 plum tomatoes, cored
2 habanero chiles
8 cups chicken stock
4 limes (2 peeled of pith and roughly chopped, 2 halved lengthwise and very thinly sliced crosswise)
1 tsp. dried thyme
1 tsp. dried oregano
8 bone-in, skinless chicken thighs
Kosher salt and freshly ground black pepper, to taste
1 cup finely chopped white onion

Instructions

1.   Heat oil in a 12" skillet over medium-high heat. Working in batches, add tortilla strips, and fry, tossing, until crisp and browned, about 3 minutes. Using a slotted spoon, transfer to paper towels to drain; set aside.

2.   Arrange an oven rack 4" from broiler and heat broiler to high. Place tomatoes, garlic, and chiles on a foil-lined baking sheet, and broil, turning as needed, until blackened all over, about 15 minutes for tomatoes, 10 minutes for garlic, and 6 minutes for chiles. Remove stems and seeds from chiles, and thinly slice; set aside. Transfer tomatoes and garlic to a food processor along with 2 cups stock and 2 peeled limes; puree until smooth, at least 2 minutes.

3.   Pour through a fine strainer into a 6-qt. saucepan and stir in remaining stock. Add thyme, oregano, and chicken, and bring to a boil over medium-high heat; reduce heat to medium-low, and cook, covered, until chicken is cooked through, about 25 minutes. Remove chicken and transfer to a bowl to cool; remove and discard bones, and finely shred chicken. Set chicken aside, and season soup with salt and pepper.

4.   To serve, divide shredded chicken, fried tortillas, onion, sliced chiles, and sliced limes among serving bowls, and then ladle soup into bowls, and serve immediately.

Arroz a la Mexicana
Mexican Rice

Yield: serves 6-8
Ingredients
2 cups chicken stock
2 ripe tomatoes, cored and chopped
2 cloves garlic, smashed
1/2 small yellow onion, chopped
2 tbsp. canola oil
1 cup long grain white rice
Kosher salt and freshly ground black pepper, to taste
Instructions
1.   Place stock, tomatoes, 1 clove garlic, and onion in a blender and purée until smooth; set tomato mixture aside.
2.   Heat oil in a 4-qt. saucepan over medium-high heat; add remaining garlic and rice and cook, stirring occasionally, until golden brown, about 6 minutes. Stir in tomato mixture, season with salt and pepper, and reduce heat to low. Cook, covered, until rice is tender and has absorbed all liquid, 25-30 minutes. Remove from heat and let sit, covered, for 10 minutes. Gently fluff the rice with a fork.

Asado de Bodas
Pork in Red Chile Sauce

Yield: serves 8-10
Ingredients
8 dried New Mexico chiles, stemmed and seeded
2 dried guajillo chiles, stemmed and seeded
1/2 cup almonds
1/2 cup unsalted peanuts
1/2 cup raisins
1/4 tsp. ground cumin
1/4 tsp. ground cinnamon
3 cloves garlic, smashed
2 whole cloves
2 oz. Mexican chocolate, such as Ibarra, roughly chopped
1/4 small yellow onion, chopped
Kosher salt and freshly ground black pepper, to taste
1 tbsp. canola oil
2 lb. boneless pork shoulder, cut into 1" chunks

Instructions

1.   Heat chiles in a 12″ skillet over high heat and cook, turning, until lightly toasted, about 5 minutes; transfer to a blender. Return skillet to heat and add almonds and peanuts; cook, stirring often, until lightly toasted, about 3 minutes. Transfer nuts to blender, reserving skillet, and add raisins, cumin, cinnamon, garlic, cloves, chocolate, onion, and 5 cups boiling water; season with salt and pepper, and puree until smooth. Set sauce aside.

2.   Heat oil in skillet over medium-high heat. Season pork with salt and pepper and, working in batches, add to skillet and cook, turning as needed, until pork is browned on all sides, about 12 minutes.

3.   Stir the sauce into the pork and bring to a boil. Reduce the heat to medium-low and cook, stirring occasionally, until pork is tender, about 1 hour.

NOTES

Paletas de Tamarindo y Chile
Tamarind Chile Ice Pops

Yield: makes 8 Ice Pops
Ingredients
6 oz. tamarind concentrate
1/3 cup sugar
1/4 tsp. ancho chile powder
Instructions

1.   Bring tamarind, sugar, and 3 cups water to a boil in a 2-qt. saucepan. Cook, whisking constantly, until sugar and tamarind dissolve, about 3 minutes. Transfer tamarind mixture to a bowl and refrigerate until chilled.

2.   Whisk in the chile powder and pour into six 3-oz. ice-pop molds. Transfer molds to the freezer and freeze until slushy, about 1 hour.

3.   Insert a popsicle stick into each mold and freeze until pops are solid, about 3 hours more. To release ice pops from molds, run the bottom of the molds briefly under warm water.

Paletas de Arroz con Leche
Rice Pudding Ice Pops

Yield: makes 12 ice pops
Ingredients
3 cups whole milk
1 vanilla bean, halved lengthwise and beans scraped
1 cup short- or medium-grain rice
2 sticks cinnamon
1 (14-oz.) can sweetened condensed milk mixed with 2 cups water
2 tsp. vanilla extract
1/4 tsp. kosher salt
1/4 tsp. ground cinnamon

Instructions

1.   Bring whole milk, 1 1/4 cups water, and vanilla beans to a simmer in a 4-qt. pot over medium-low heat. Stir in rice and cinnamon sticks and cook, stirring occasionally, until rice is tender, 20–30 minutes. Remove cinnamon sticks and stir in condensed milk mixture, vanilla extract, and salt. Simmer until the rice has absorbed most of the liquid, 10–15 minutes more. Remove pan from heat, stir in ground cinnamon, and let cool slightly.

2.   Transfer mixture to twelve 3-oz. ice-pop molds. Transfer molds to the freezer and freeze until slushy, about 1 hour. Insert a Popsicle stick into each mold and freeze until pops are solid, about 3 hours more. To release ice pops from molds, run the bottom of the molds briefly under warm water.

Paletas de Pina
Pineapple Ice Pops

Yield: makes 8 ice pops
Ingredients
1 cup sugar
4 cups minced fresh pineapple
Instructions
1. Bring sugar and 1 cup water to a boil in a 1-qt. saucepan and stir until sugar dissolves. Transfer mixture to a bowl and refrigerate until chilled.
2. Put the chilled mixture and half of the pineapple into a blender; puree. Set a fine sieve over a bowl and strain pureed pineapple mixture, discarding solids. Stir the remaining pineapple into the mixture and pour into eight 3-oz. ice-pop molds.
3. Transfer molds to the freezer and freeze until slushy, about 1 hour. Insert a popsicle stick into each mold and freeze until pops are solid, about 3 hours more. To release ice pops from molds, run the bottom of the molds briefly under warm water.

Paletas de Fresas y Crema
Strawberries and Cream Ice Pops

Yield: makes four ice pops
Ingredients
1 lb. hulled strawberries
1/3 cup sugar
1/4 cup heavy cream
1 tbsp. fresh lemon juice
Instructions

1.   Purée strawberries in a blender. Set a fine strainer over a bowl; strain strawberry purée, discarding solids. Whisk in sugar, heavy cream, and lemon juice until sugar dissolves. Pour strawberry mixture into four 3-oz. ice-pop molds.

2.   Transfer molds to the freezer and freeze until slushy, about 1 hour. Insert a Popsicle stick into each mold and freeze until pops are solid, about 3 hours more. To release ice pops from molds, run the bottom of the molds briefly under warm water.

Paletas de Mango con Chile
Mango Chile Ice Pops

Yield: makes 8 ICE POPS
Ingredients
1 cup store-bought mango juice or nectar
1/4 cup sugar
2 tsp. fresh lemon juice
1 tsp. ancho chile powder
1 large mango, peeled, seeded, and cut into small cubes
Instructions
1.   Heat mango juice, sugar, lemon juice, and 1/2 cup water in a 1-qt. saucepan over medium-high heat and stir until sugar dissolves. Transfer mixture to a bowl and refrigerate until chilled.
2.   Stir chile powder and cubed mango into the chilled mixture and pour into eight 3-oz. ice-pop molds. Insert a Popsicle stick into each mold and freeze until pops are solid, about 3 hours more. To release ice pops from molds, run the bottom of the molds briefly under cold water.

Some Random Pics...

Horchata Blanca (White Rice Drink)

Yield: serves 8
Ingredients
1/3 cup medium or long grain rice
1 (1") piece Mexican cinnamon
1/2 tsp. vanilla
12 oz. evaporated milk
14 oz. condensed milk
Freshly ground Mexican cinnamon, to garnish
Instructions

1.   Toast the cinnamon and rice in a heavy skillet over medium-low heat until they release a nutty aroma. Remove from heat and transfer onto a blender; blend into a fine powder. Add the vanilla, evaporated milk, condensed milk, and 4 cups of water. Strain mixture through a wet cheesecloth into a serving pitcher. Chill completely, and serve over ice, or heat and serve warm. Top with freshly ground cinnamon right before serving.

Horchata de Arroz Tostado
Toasted Rice Drink

Yield: serves 4

Ingredients

1/3 cup medium or long grain rice

1 (1-inch) piece Mexican cinnamon

1/4 cup granulated sugar

1/2 tsp. vanilla

freshly ground Mexican cinnamon, to garnish

Instructions

1.   Toast the cinnamon and rice in a heavy skillet over medium-low heat until they release a nutty aroma. Remove from heat and transfer onto a blender; blend into a fine powder. Add 2 cups of water, the sugar, and vanilla, and blend well. Strain mixture through a wet cheesecloth into a large serving pitcher and stir in 2 more cups of water. Chill, and serve over ice. Top with freshly ground cinnamon right before serving.

Horchata de Arroz con Almendras Almond Rice Drink

Yield: serves 4-6

Ingredients

1/3 cup long grain rice

1 (1-inch) piece Mexican cinnamon

2 (1-inch) strips lime or lemon zest plus grated lime zest, for garnish

1 cup whole blanched almonds, lightly toasted

1 1/2 cups sugar

1/2 tsp. pure vanilla extract

Instructions

1.   ut the rice in a blender or spice grinder and process until it's completely pulverized, with a flourlike texture. Transfer into a large container and add the cinnamon, lime zest, and almonds. Stir in 2 cups water, cover, and let sit overnight.

2.   Transfer the mixture to a blender and blend until as smooth as possible. Add 2 more cups of water, mix, and strain into a pitcher through a sieve or colander lined with damp cheesecloth, pouring carefully and slowly and pressing the solids with the back of a wooden spoon to extract as much liquid as possible. If you have lots of bits remaining in the cheesecloth, blend again with some of the strained liquid, then strain over the damp cheesecloths once again. Stir in the sugar and vanilla, then taste and add more sugar if you like. Serve over ice, garnished with fresh lime zest.

Horchata de Melon Cantaloupe Seed Drink

Yield: serves 6
Ingredients
Seeds from 1 medium cantaloupe (about 1/2 cup)
1/4 tsp. vanilla extract
Pinch of salt
Honey, to taste
Instructions
1.   In a blender, grind the melon seeds with 2 cups of water until as smooth as possible. Pour mixture through a strainer into a large pitcher. Return the seed bits left on the strainer to the blender and mix with 2 more cups water, vanilla, salt, and honey, to taste. Strain this mixture into the pitcher as well. Stir well, and add more honey to taste if desired. Serve chilled over ice.

Horchata de Moras
Berry Rice Drink

Yield: serves 6
Ingredients
1/3 cup medium or long grained white rice
2 cups mixed berries
Sugar, to taste
Instructions
1.   Soak the rice in 1 cup of water for 15 minutes, then strain. In a blender, blend the rice with the berries and 2 cups of water until smooth. Strain the mixture through a damp cheesecloth or fine mesh strainer into a large pitcher and mix with 3 more cups of water. Add sugar to taste. Serve chilled over ice.

Horchata de Chabacano Apricot Rice Drink

Yield: serves 6
Ingredients
1 lb. fresh apricots, pitted and quartered
1/2 cup sugar, plus more to taste
1/3 cup medium or long grained rice
1/2 tsp. vanilla
Instructions
1.   In a small saucepan over medium heat, stir the apricots and 1/2 cup sugar until the apricots are soft and a bubbling sauce has formed. Remove from heat and let cool.
2.   Meanwhile, soak the rice in 1 cup of water until the apricots have cooled completely, then strain the rice. Transfer the rice and fruit mixture to a blender and blend with 3 cups of water water and the vanilla. Strain mixture through a wet cheesecloth into a large serving pitcher, then mix in another 2 cups of water. Taste, and add more sugar if desired. Chill completely, and serve over ice.

Chico

Ingredients
2 oz. gin or silver tequila
2 oz. blackberry liqueur
1 oz. simple syrup
1/2 oz. fresh lemon juice
Club soda, to taste
Instructions
1. Fill a highball glass with ice. Add the gin, liqueur, simple syrup, and lemon juice; top off with club soda. Stir.

Some Random Pics...

MORE OF MY BOOK'S

FOOD of CULTURE

By Chef Peter Ingrasselino

Food of Culture
"World of Meats,
Red, White & Yellow"

A reality series of cookbooks

By Chef Peter Ingrasselino

Food of Culture
"World of Gluten Free"

A reality series of cookbooks

By Chef Peter Ingrasselino

Food of Culture
"Sweets and Treats"
Family Traditions

A reality series of cookbooks

By Chef Peter Ingrasselino

Food of Culture
"World of BBQ"

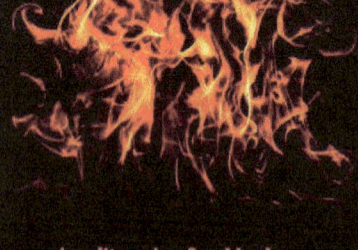

A reality series of cookbooks

Author: Chef Peter Ingrasselino™

Food of Culture
World of Greens, Beans,
& Leafy things...

A reality series of cookbooks

By Chef Peter Ingrasselino

Food of Culture
The Waters of the World

A reality series of cookbooks

By Chef Peter Ingrasselino

Food of Culture
"World of Pasta and Noodles"

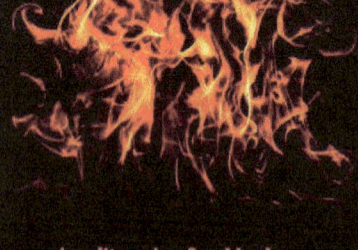

A reality series of cookbooks

By Chef Peter Ingrasselino

Food of Culture
"World of Veganism"

A reality series of cookbooks

By Chef Peter Ingrasselino

Marketing For Life

a reality book

Author Peter Ingrasselino

Food of Culture
"World of Christmas"

A reality series of cookbooks
By Chef Peter Ingrasselino

TIME

A Reality Book
Author: Peter Ingrasselino™

Food of Culture
"World of Coal Cooking"

A reality series of cookbooks
By Chef Peter Ingrasselino

Food of Culture
"World of Dressings &
Marinades"

A reality series of cookbooks
By Chef Peter Ingrasselino

Food of Culture
"Caribbean World"

A reality series of cookbooks
By Chef Peter Ingraselino

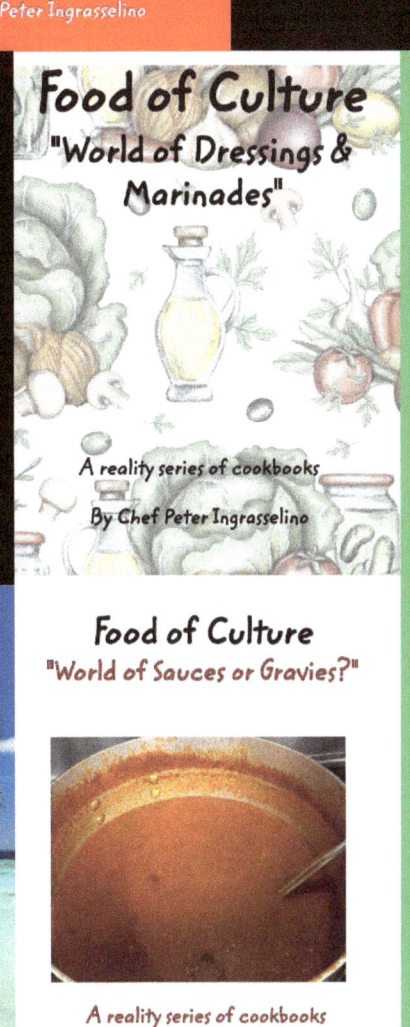

Food of Culture
"World of Sauces or Gravies?"

A reality series of cookbooks
By Chef Peter Ingrasselino

This is that Section that I mention People throughout my Career

To ALL of you and you know who you are, that have had a impact on my career path Good and Bad, Supportive and Not, Hired me and Fired me. ALL of you have helped me to be who I am today and I Thank You. If I did not have the experiences in my life with ALL of you, I would not be where I am in my career today, without any of you being there along the way, so Thank You for everything that I have learned and still to come.

I am still faced with challenges to overcome but everyday I thank of ALL of you and what I have learned to remind me and give me the strength to carry on and to create the taste for more to come. I find myself more eager to pass on what I have learned so that others have a more positive experience then the school of hard knocks that I have done. The path I chose was not easy, lots of time lost, friendships and relationships lost, quality time just vanished, and before I knew it people have passed away wishing that they could see me today. So now is the time for me to pass what I have learned and hopefully what I am going to pass on moving forward will help others in this industry be smarter, wiser and not make the mistakes that I have made along my way. This is just the begging to my series of books that will continue to tell a culinary story of a Chef that has a true meaning of this Industry facts. So once again to ALL of you, Thank You Once Again!!!

INDEX

I am leaving our Mexican journey, hopefully
they will let me back into the United States...

A reality series of cookbooks
AUTHOR: Peter Ingrasselino™
www.ingrasselinoproducts.com